The Croscups' Painted Parlour

VICTORIA BAKER

The Croscups' Painted Parlour

NATIONAL
GALLERY
OF
CANADA
OTTAWA
1990

DESIGN: Frank Newfeld

Available from bookseller, or from
The Bookstore, National Gallery of
Canada, 380 Sussex Drive, Box 427,
Station A, Ottawa K1N 9N4

Canadian Cataloguing in Publication Data

National Gallery of Canada.
The Croscups' painted parlour. –

Text by Victoria Baker.
Issued also in French under title:
Le salon peint des Croscup.
ISBN 0-88884-597-9

1. Mural painting and decoration,
Canadian.
2. Croscup, William, 1811–1888.
3. Croscup, Hannah Amelia, 1820–1913.
I. Baker, Victoria A., 1952–   II. Title.

ND2643 .05 N37 1990
751.7'3   CIP 90–099154–2

FRONT COVER:

Unknown artist
*Atlantic Harbour Scene with
Ship Launching* 1846–48
(detail of north wall, pl.2)

FRONTISPIECE:

Unknown artist
*Queen Victoria and Prince Albert
Presenting Princess Victoria,
Prince Edward, and Princess Alice
to Louis-Philippe, King of the French*
1846–48
(detail of east wall, pl.3)

BACK COVER:

Unknown artist
*Peter I Square, Saint Petersburg,
Russia* 1846–48
(detail of west wall, pl.1)

PHOTOGRAPH CREDITS

11, 15   Courtesy Michael Bird and Terry
Kobayashi
13   Renate Deppe, courtesy Art Gallery of
Nova Scotia, Halifax
46, 48, 49   Cora Greenaway, Halifax
12, 19   Cora Greenaway, courtesy Art
Gallery of Nova Scotia, Halifax
8   Helga Photo Studio, Upper Montclair,
New Jersey, courtesy of *The Magazine
Antiques*
18   Hodson Studio, courtesy Mrs Alix
Gronau, Picton, Ontario
14   Aubrey P. Janion, Historic American
Buildings Survey, Library of Congress,
Washington, D.C.
47   Joe Knycha, Middleton, Nova Scotia
7   The Marblehead Historical Society,
Marblehead, Massachusetts
29, 30, 31   The Metropolitan Museum of
Art, New York
26   Musée de Besançon, France
17   Musée des arts décoratifs, Paris
3, 20, 21, 23, 27, 28, 32, 34, 38, 39, 40, 43
National Archives of Canada, Ottawa
Plates I-IV, frontispiece, 1, 2, 4, 35, 41, 42,
50, 51, 52   National Gallery of Canada,
Ottawa
45   Notman Photographic Archives,
McCord Museum of Canadian History,
Montreal
24, 25   Réunion des musées nationaux,
Paris
9, 10   Scott Robson, courtesy Nova Scotia
Museum, Halifax
22, 36, 37   Royal Ontario Museum,
Toronto
5, 33   Society for the Preservation of New
England Antiquities, Boston
6   Ramsay Traquair Archive, Canadian
Architecture Collection, Blackader-
Lauterman Library of Architecture and
Arts, McGill University, Montreal
44   Upper Canada Village, The
St. Lawrence Parks Commission,
Morrisburg, Ontario
16   V.I.P. Photography, Lebanon,
Connecticut

Contents

Foreword

❋

THE CROSCUP ROOM, as it has become known, originally was the ground floor parlour of the Croscup house, located in Karsdale, Nova Scotia, on the north shore of the Annapolis Basin a few miles west of Annapolis Royal. It is named after the first owners, William Croscup (1811–1888) and his wife Hannah Amelia Schaffner (1820–1913), for whom the room was decorated some time between 1846 and 1848 by an unidentified artist. Featuring a remarkable group of scenic murals set in an architectural framework painted in simulated marble and fine wood grains, it is recognized today as an outstanding example of Canadian provincial interior decorative painting from the pre-Confederation period.

Although the painted room was familiar to the friends and relations of the Croscups and later tenants, it was not until the 1960s that it was brought to the attention of other Nova Scotians by local historian Cora Greenaway, who has written warmly about her experience in the Preface. Mrs Greenaway was first taken to see the painted room in 1961 by Mrs Marion Beard, great-granddaughter of William and Hannah Croscup. Shortly afterwards she broadcast news of her discovery in a CBC radio program out of Halifax.

Her pioneering effort to increase public awareness of the historic and artistic value of this exceptional decorated interior was complemented by the activities of the Heritage Trust of Nova Scotia. Its 1972 publication *Seasoned Timbers: A Sampling of Historic Buildings Unique to Western Nova Scotia* included a text on the Croscup house by Cora Greenaway. In 1973 the Croscup room became the object of national interest when, through photographic reproductions, the murals were highlighted in the travelling exhibition, *A People's Art: Naïve Art in Canada*, organized by J. Russell Harper for the National Gallery of Canada.

With the growing realization of the cultural importance of the Croscup room, concern over the declining physical state of the paintings also developed, and the owners, Mr and Mrs Roy A. Hall, sought to find a way to ensure their preservation. As a result, in 1976 the room was acquired by the National Gallery of Canada, complete with painted plaster walls, wood floor, fireplace, doors, windows, and architectural trim. In a complex operation, detailed in the Appendix, it was transferred, restored, and reassembled as a major and unique installation in the Canadian gallery of early Maritime art. The conservation team from the Master of Art Conservation program at Queen's University, supervised by Ian Hodkinson, Professor of Fine Art Conservation, along with the staff of the Gallery's Restoration and Conservation Laboratory and Technical Services Workshop, are to be commended for their exceptional achievement. My thanks, too, to Victoria Baker, Assistant Curator of Canadian Art, who has written so knowledgeably on the history and background of the room, and to Charles C. Hill, Curator of Canadian Art, who initiated the idea for this book.

DR SHIRLEY L. THOMSON

Director
National Gallery of Canada

Preface

I N 1961, Mrs Marion Beard invited me to see her great-grandmother's home with its "painted room." On a particularly bright day in October we drove to Karsdale, a tiny but historic village on the shores of the Annapolis Basin in Nova Scotia. The house was a modest dwelling with a central gable and front door. Mrs Beard led me to a front room which was in semi-darkness. She raised the blinds and the sunlight revealed an unexpected and incredible display of superb wall paintings. The impression on me was indelible. Each scene was different and depicted urban views and landscapes, the launching of a ship, portraits, and a Micmac family. The varnish over the paintings had darkened with age. The surface was grimy and dusty and in several places the paint was flaking. Even so, nothing could detract from the stunning impact of this marvellous room.

The "painted room" had been the parlour, the best room, but was now only a storeroom. In one corner stood two sacks of grain or feed, in another a stack of boxes. A pair of skis rested against one of the painted walls. Instead of being a room full of treasures it was a forlorn room. A flood of questions raced through my mind. How could such a valuable asset be unknown except to the family of the original owners, William and Hannah

Amelia Croscup? When and by whom were these walls decorated, and how could they be brought to the attention of the public for preservation and display? Finding the answers to these questions became a personal crusade, because, at the time, my anxiety to preserve this unique room was not shared by others. In the 1960s, the value of local history was the concern of only a few, and the Nova Scotia government had no department of cultural affairs.

Marion Beard, who was born in 1902, recalled with pleasure her experiences as a little girl visiting her great-grandmother Hannah Amelia Croscup (1820–1913). She remembers Hannah Croscup as a formidable old lady, short of stature, dressed in black, with a lace cap on her head and a cane in one hand. Marion, a tomboy, was not her great-grandmother's idea of a perfectly behaved little girl. The "painted room" was strictly out-of-bounds to children, who were only allowed to stand on the threshold and look in. At times temptation proved too strong for at least one small child. W. Reginald Bishop (1891–1987), Marion's brother, told me that when he was about four or five years old, the minute he was sure that Mrs Croscup was busily occupied elsewhere, he would sneak into the forbidden room "to look at the pictures." What a delight that must have been for a small boy in the days when there was no cinema or television and few books. I asked Mr Bishop if he had a likeness of his great-grandmother as a young woman. He shook his head and said "No, but she is on the wall." The young woman to the left of the fireplace holding a small child represents Hannah Amelia Croscup. The infant is her first child, Lucretia, born in 1846.

Family oral history has it that one stormy night in the 1840s a stranger knocked on the door asking for asylum. He said he was an Englishman, that he had deserted his ship, and that he had no money. Could he decorate the parlour for Mrs Croscup in return for his board and lodging? No one has remembered the painter's name and he did not sign his work. He left the following spring to return to England. How had this talented artist come to be in Karsdale? Had he been a victim of the press gangs that were prevalent in England at the time? Was he an apprentice painter? The whole story may never be known, and perhaps the mystery enhances the charm of the Croscup room.

In Hannah Amelia's lifetime the painted room was a legend in the family and a great source of pride. In 1961, shortly before her death, I met Mrs Mary Bent (1880–1962), the only child of Lucretia Croscup (1846–1906) and Captain Israel Delap (1841–1891). She was frail and her mind cloudy, but when she was shown snapshots of the room, she recognized it immediately and identified the lady on the painted overmantel, pointing her finger at it and saying "Victoria." Another descendant, William Archibald Croscup, born in 1869, moved as a child to Boston with his family. In the Boston directories of 1891–95 he is listed as a "fresco painter." Did he remember the Croscup room when he chose his profession?

The house passed out of the family in 1920 and the parlour was no longer regarded as a special room, though it was never abused or papered over. It simply did not have the same family value for the new owners. By the 1970s, the murals had deteriorated alarmingly but my ceaseless efforts to arouse interest in them seemed doomed to failure. And so it was with mixed feelings of sadness and relief for me when the National Gallery learned of the room, purchased it and restored it, and eventually installed it in its present location. It was clearly the right solution, but after so many years of involvement I felt it as a personal loss. It was then that I began serious research into interior decorative painting in Nova Scotia. Many examples have survived in the province, but there are only two rooms completely decorated with scenic murals, and both have a connection with the Croscup room.

In January 1981, a room decorated with scenic murals was uncovered in a house in South Williamston, and in March of the same year, news came of the existence of another painted room in Bear River. The house in South Williamston was built in 1864 by John Schaffner and his son William Judson. In 1867, Mary Hester, second daughter of Hannah Amelia and William Croscup, married her distant cousin William Judson and came to live in the house. It was there that Marion Beard's mother was born in 1871. The room, perhaps decorated to please the bride, is much less sophisticated than the Croscups' parlour, but it is still captivating in its freshness. In the Bear River room, one small wall panel has been stripped, revealing a landscape containing a house with a portico and with two cows and a horse in the foreground. In style it resembles the Croscup room and may have been painted about 1850.

During the first half of the nineteenth century the Croscups lived in the same general area. By 1840 they began to settle elsewhere and today there are few descendants in the Granville area. They can be found in Maine and other parts of New England, California, Ontario, and Quebec.

William and Hannah Amelia Croscup lived in the same house all their married life. They both died there, and were probably laid out in the painted parlour. After a long period of neglect, expert and sympathetic restoration has given new life to these wonderful murals. They shine again as brightly as when they were first painted in the mid-nineteenth century by an unknown artist for William and Hannah Amelia Croscup.

CORA GREENAWAY

Dartmouth, Nova Scotia

Acknowledgements

AN INTRIGUING PUZZLE, as well as a visual delight, the Croscup family's painted parlour has sparked the interest of several researchers before me, all intent on unravelling the mystery of this unique room and assessing its historical and artistic significance. Gilbert Gignac and Jeanne L'Espérance deserve special credit for their seminal iconographic research reported in the 1982 article for *The Journal of Canadian Art History*. I am equally indebted to Cora Greenaway for sharing the results of her pioneering work on the subject. For their expertise and advice I am also grateful to Gilbert Gignac, Documentary Art Custodian, Documentary Art and Photography Division, National Archives of Canada; Marie Elwood, Curator of History, Nova Scotia Museum; Felicity Leung, Historian, Historical Research Branch, Canadian Parks Service, Environment Canada; Ruth Holmes Whitehead, Curatorial Assistant, Ethnology, Nova Scotia Museum; Dr Charles Armour, Head Archivist, Dalhousie University Archives; and Barbara J. Christie, Research Associate, Nova Scotia Museum. I also wish to thank my predecessor Ross Fox, now Curator at the Art Gallery of Hamilton; Glen Wright, Archivist, National Archives of Canada; Jacqueline Beaudoin-Ross, Curator of Costumes and

Textiles, McCord Museum; Scott Robson, Curator of Historic Houses and Furnishings, Nova Scotia Museum; Professor Michael Bird, Renison College, University of Waterloo; Susan Foshay, Exhibitions Curator, Art Gallery of Nova Scotia; Marven Moore, Curator, Maritime Museum of the Atlantic; Allison Eckardt Ledes, Associate Editor, *The Magazine Antiques*; Barbara Scott, Historian; Mrs John P. Hunt, Jr., Marblehead Historical Society; Lorna Condon, Associate Archivist, Society for the Preservation of New England Antiquities; Judith Johnson, Connecticut Historical Museum and Library; Wayne Duford, Photographic Collections Analyst, Architectural History Branch, Canadian Parks Service; Irena Murray, Chief Librarian, and Cindy Campbell, Curatorial Assistant, Canadian Architecture Collection, Blackader-Lauterman Library of Art and Architecture, McGill University; Phil Dunning, Curator, and Jack I. Schector, Librarian Archivist, Upper Canada Village. For providing access to Jeanne Minhinnick's personal research notes, my thanks to Alix Gronau.

This publication would not have been possible without the coordinated efforts of members of the National Gallery staff. I deeply appreciate the steady guidance of Charles Hill, Curator of Canadian Art and project supervisor, and the assistance of Maija Vilcins, Reference Librarian, and Barbara Ramsay-Jolicœur, Conservator of Fine Art. Special thanks go to Kathy Stone for her advice and patience in organizing the manuscript and typing the various drafts. I would also like to thank the publications staff of the Gallery, under the direction of Serge Thériault, who prepared the manuscript for publication and guided it through the stages of production: editors Norman Dahl and Jacques Pichette, picture editor Colleen Evans, production officer Jean-Guy Bergeron, and word-processing operator Micheline Ouellette. For the photographs of the Croscup murals, I am indebted to National Gallery staff photographer Charles Hupé.

VICTORIA BAKER

Assistant Curator of Canadian Art
National Gallery of Canada

❋

━●|◉|━❋━●|◉|━

The Croscups' Painted Parlour

❋

1.   2.

1

❋

The
Croscups'
Painted Parlour

❋

FAMILY CHRONICLES

1.
William Croscup (1811–1888),
photograph retouched with
charcoal pencil, 50.1 × 40.2 cm.
Collection: National Gallery
of Canada.

2.
Hannah Amelia Schaffner Croscup
(1820–1913), ferrotype, heightened,
9.0 × 5.6 cm (image), dated
c. 1879–83.
The photograph was found behind
the mantel in the Croscup parlour
when it was being dismantled
by the National Gallery.
Collection: National Gallery
of Canada.

THE PRECISE DATE of the project to decorate the front parlour of the Croscup family home in Karsdale, Nova Scotia, and the circumstances surrounding it are undocumented. It is known that William Croscup, the original homeowner for whom the murals were painted, was a relatively prosperous farmer and shipbuilder from a Loyalist family *(fig. 1)*. His grandparents, Ludwick and Mary (née Kraus) Croscup, had first come to Digby, Nova Scotia, from New York some time in 1783 and had moved across the Annapolis Basin to Lower Granville by 21 January 1784. Ludwick Croscup (originally "Krauskopf") and his wife were German Lutherans who chose to become British citizens and adopt the Anglican faith after moving to New York City shortly before their marriage on 3 March 1762. A substantial landowner and farmer in New York, Ludwick Croscup was probably lured to Nova Scotia by the large tracts of land available for settlement after the American Revolution.[1]

From his arrival in Granville in 1784, until his death in 1819, Ludwick prospered as a farmer and man of property, buying and selling numerous local plots of land.[2] His second son, Daniel, followed in his footsteps as did his grandson, William, who also made his living as a shipbuilder and investor. William Croscup was born on an unspecified day in November 1811 and grew up in the Granville area.[3] On 15 August 1844 he married Hannah Amelia Schaffner,[4] the daughter of James Schaffner, descendant

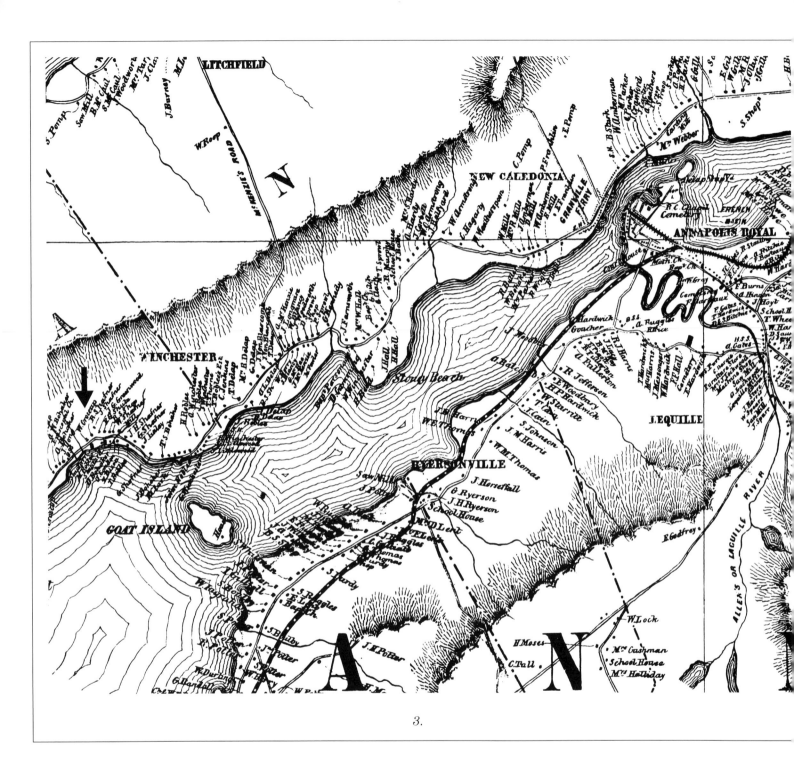

3.
Topographical township map of Annapolis County, N.S., from actual surveys made, drawn, and engraved by Ambrose F. Church, 24 March 1864. The arrow on the left indicates the location of the Croscup house.

Collection: Cartographic and Architectural Archives Division, National Archives of Canada.

4.

4.
South façade of the Croscup-Hall House, Karsdale, N.S. The two ground floor windows on the left, providing a view across the Annapolis Basin, mark the location of the painted parlour. Built about 1845, the house remained in the hands of the Croscup family until 1920, when it was bought by Noble Wheelock, father of Mrs Roy A. Hall, one of the present residents. Mr and Mrs Hall sold the parlour to the National Gallery of Canada in 1976.

of another regionally well-known Loyalist family of German origin, and his cousin, Esther Croscup.[5] Born on 8 June 1820,[6] Hannah was also a Granville native (fig. 2). Like her husband, she remained a resident of this part of Nova Scotia until her death on 10 January 1913 at 92,[7] some twenty-five years after William was buried on 7 March 1888.[8]

In January 1845, five months to the day after his marriage, William purchased from Robert H. Foster a 250-acre waterfront lot at Lower Granville, as this sector of the greater district of Granville was then called.[9] It was here within the boundaries of the modern community of Karsdale that the young couple chose to settle (fig. 3). As no mention of a house is made in the documentation of the transaction with Foster, it cannot be confirmed whether a house was included in the land sale. It seems plausible, however, that the house found on this property today was built by William around 1845, a construction date which accords with its design (fig. 4). Typical of Maritime vernacular frame dwellings popular in the Annapolis Valley in the 1840s, the Croscup house is a simple, storey-and-a-half rectangular structure clad in painted clapboard, with a centre-hall plan, central chimney, pitched roof covered with shingles, and partial basement.[10] Although similar to the older Cape Cod type of cottage imported to Nova Scotia from New England in the late 1700s, it is distinguished from it by a broad triangular dormer integrated into the roofline and a large, round-headed Georgian window. Originally the house is said to have had a front porch with pillars and a second-storey balcony off the upper window. The small east wing is a later addition.[11]

Iconographic analysis of the murals suggests that it was not long after the Croscups had moved into their new home that the interior of the parlour was decorated. According to one story passed down to certain Croscup descendants, the artist was "an English sailor who used to paint ships' cabins in the summer and do interior decorating in the winter."[12] Another family tradition, similar in nature, attributes the work to an Englishman said to have been forcibly enlisted in London to crew a ship bound for Canada. Deserting his vessel at Annapolis Royal, the recalcitrant sailor reportedly found refuge for the winter in the household of William and Hannah Amelia Croscup. In return for the couple's hospitality, he painted their parlour before departing for England in the spring.[13]

This story is analogous to those surrounding the otherwise undocumented histories of a number of North American painted rooms, which similarly recall the brief visit of an artistically inclined foreign traveller, variously described as a British or French soldier, sailor, deserter, prisoner, spy, or intemperate vagabond.[14] Though romanticized, the tale of the Croscup artist may, like these others, have some basis in fact, for much of the ornamental painting executed in North American homes before 1850, notably in rural communities, was the work of itinerant painter-decorators. Familiar with all types of painting, these skilled craftsmen generally travelled door to door through town and country in search of customers. For room and board or a modest wage they would paint house interiors as well as carriages, sleighs, signs, furniture, and sometimes even portraits. The unconventional nature of their professional lives no doubt gave rise to rumours in provincial circles, many now become legend.

"FANCY ARCHITECTURAL PAINTING"

The decorative scheme of the Croscup parlour was evidently planned with careful consideration of the social function as well as the architectural realities of the space. As the designated main parlour, this room was an important area of activity in the household. In early Victorian times, visitors would have been received and elegantly entertained here in nineteenth-century style with teas, polite conversation, recitations, parlour games and, perhaps, an occasional music recital. Here, too, family members would have engaged in such pastimes as reading and needlework. Not surprisingly, it was this part of the house, serving in the mid-nineteenth century as both social centre and private oasis, that was the most lavishly decorated and furnished.

By choosing to paint this small domestic interior, measuring less than four metres by five, with an elaborate series of large scenic murals, the Croscup artist was responding as much to the problem of limited space as to the dictates of function and period fashions. Through painterly illusion the spatial restrictions of the room were overcome. The murals, covering the walls from floor to ceiling around the windows, doors, and mantel, help open the interior visually. The framing woodwork and the illusionistic painting of a red curtain draped in swags on a black rod running along the top and the sides of each painting reinforce the effect of a room full of windows opening onto the outside world by calling attention to the solid wall and mediating between real and pictorial space. The clever interplay between tangible and imaginary worlds established by this decorative scheme is also significant in terms of the iconographic program. In the way the doors and windows provide glimpses of the interior and exterior of the house, the murals present selected views both of the immediate world of the Croscup family and the wider universe outside Nova Scotia.

The practice of embellishing domestic interiors with painted decorations dates in North America from the early eighteenth century and was particularly popular during the first half of the nineteenth century. Besides easel paintings on canvas or panel, of which mostly portraits have survived, colonial taste equally favoured what was termed "fancy architectural painting." The latter category includes stencilled and freehand repeat patterns

5.

applied to walls and floors, imitation woodgrain and marble finishes for chimney mantels and secondary woodwork, as well as more elaborate landscape and genre pieces to adorn walls and overmantel areas. European – principally English and French – decorative traditions and styles significantly influenced North American artisans and their patrons. Painted pictorial wall and overmantel panels, for example, which were integral elements of English room decor by the late seventeenth century, became fashionable in British North America from the second quarter of the eighteenth century.[15] The painted overmantel panel in the parlour of the Waid-Tinker house in Old Lyme, Connecticut, is a typical example of this trend in American provincial decorative painting *(fig. 5)*.[16] North American interest in such decoration was further stimulated by the work of leading European designers such as the British Neo-Classical architect and interior decorator,

6.
Parlour with wood panelling,
Maison Estèbe, 92 rue St. Pierre,
Quebec City, built in 1752. The
photograph was taken in the 1920s
by Ramsay Traquair. Collection:
Ramsay Traquair Archive, Canadian
Architecture Collection,
Blackader-Lauterman Library,
McGill University, Montreal.

6.

Robert Adam (1728–1792), who advocated the extensive use of ornamental wall painting.[17]

The popular vogue for patterned wallpapers, which developed in New England in the eighteenth century and in British North America in the early nineteenth century, also had an impact on the practice and evolution of interior decorative painting. Progressive improvements in the fabrication and printing of paper wall hangings from the late 1600s fostered the gradual abandonment of traditional materials – such as wood, leather, and sumptuous fabrics – to decorate European and, in time, North American room interiors. Even in Quebec, where the tradition of finishing ecclesiastical, civic, and domestic interiors with carved and painted wood panels continued through the nineteenth century *(fig. 6)*, printed wallpapers became a viable alternative for decorating domestic interiors from as early as the eighteenth century.[18] It was after 1800, however, that their popularity in Upper Canada and the Atlantic colonies, as well as Quebec, began to grow significantly.

Besides a wide variety of repeat patterns – including floral,

7.

7.
Roman Ruins, a Jackson of Battersea wallpaper printed in England in 1756–90 and installed in the Jeremiah Lee Mansion, Marblehead, Mass. According to Houel's *Journal des Inventions* (Paris, 1795), "… for the view, the cleanliness, the freshness and the elegance, … [wall]papers are preferable to the rich materials of the past; they do not allow any access to insects, and when they are varnished, they retain all the vivacity and charm of their colours for a long time … wallpapers add to our interest in life, and deserve to be regarded as a manufactured object of prime necessity." Collection: Marblehead Historical Society, Marblehead, Mass.

geometric, architectural, and imitation wood, fabric, marble, caning, and stucco prints – by the late eighteenth century wallpapers featuring landscape and figurative compositions after the manner of tapestry and wall panel paintings were being produced by English and French as well as American manufacturers *(fig. 7)*. French wallpapers were especially prized luxury items in the United States and British North America in the half century after the American revolution.

French pictorial, or scenic, wallpapers featuring larger and more ambitious designs than earlier paperhangings were created to entirely cover the walls of a room, usually with a sequential series of continuous or thematically related pictures *(fig. 8)*.[19] Despite their high price and the installation difficulties involved, imported scenic wallpapers found their way into a significant number of North American parlours, dining rooms, and foyers, including some in Nova Scotian homes. For instance, the Joseph Dufour scenic paper illustrating the story of *Telemachus in*

8.

8.
"The Lindens," central entrance hall, main level, built in 1754 for Robert Hooper in Danvers, Mass., moved in the 1930s to Washington, D.C. At the left is the Dufour & Leroy scenic wallpaper *Les Incas*, 1826. On the right hangs the Dufour & Leroy paper, *Telemachus in the Island of Calypso*, 1823. Both sets of papers were probably installed about the mid-nineteenth century. Technical innovations by French firms permitted more durable, richly coloured and elaborately printed papers of unprecedented size and unrivalled quality. French scenic wallpapers, notably those of Jean Zuber and Joseph Dufour, entered the North American market in the early 1800s.

the Island of Calypso (first produced in 1823) was installed at considerable expense in the drawing room of Silas Hibbert Crane's home, "Hibbert's Green," built in 1823 in Economy, Nova Scotia. Crane's drawing room was specially constructed with rounded corners to receive this imported paper. As the ratio of paper to wall space was apparently miscalculated, a strip from another popular Dufour set, entitled *Les sauvages de la mer Pacifique* (also known as *The Voyage of Captain Cook*), first issued in 1821, was added over the mantel to complete the ensemble *(fig. 9)*.[20] In the home of Thomas de Wolfe in Wolfville, another set of panoramic wallpaper was installed – *Les jardins français*, initially printed in 1821 by the French firm Jean Zuber & fils *(fig. 10)*.[21]

A working relationship existed between many early British North American decorative painters and paperhangers. Not infrequently decorative painters also advertised themselves as wallpaper hangers and vendors. The business ads of Halifax-based ornamental painters John Bowles (active in 1815)[22] and George Smithers (1810–1868), in partnership with J.B. Studley (active in 1830–68),[23] provide evidence of this practice in Atlantic Canada. Similar commercial announcements may also be found in Upper and Lower Canadian newspapers during the 1800s.[24] Provincial painter-decorators were evidently sometimes asked to replace worn wallpapers or generally recreate them in paint.[25] As an elegant alternative to expensive printed wallpapers, they occasionally agreed to paint walls in imitation of imported papers using stencils or working freehand at a price more in keeping with local incomes. Writing in 1846 about "landscape painting on walls of rooms" the successful American decorative painter Rufus Porter (1792–1884) reported: "This kind of painting having been thoroughly proved to be cheaper and more durable as well as more elegant than paper hangings, there appears no other good reason than the want of competent artists to execute such work, to prevent its coming into general use, in preference."[26]

Printed wallpapers often served as the model for stencilled repeat and freehand painted wall decorations. In Canada, as in New England, stencilling appears to have enjoyed some popularity as a relatively quick means of decorating domestic interiors, judging from the nineteenth-century rooms with stencilled walls that have been discovered in Ontario *(fig. 11)*.[27]

9.

9.
Fragment of the Dufour wallpaper, *The Voyage of Captain Cook*, comprising two adjoining panels representing the inhabitants of New Caledonia, which formerly hung over the doorway in the Silas Crane house "Hibbert's Green" in Economy, N.S. Among the monied classes of Europe, scenic wallpapers provided a fashionable substitute for more expensive mural painting and stucco work. For the average North American in the early nineteenth century, however, the high cost of imported papers made the decorative work of local painter-decorators a cheaper alternative. Collection: Nova Scotia Museum, Halifax.

10.
The parlour of the
Thomas de Wolfe house,
Wolfville, N.S. (now
demolished), was decorated
with the Zuber & fils
scenic wallpaper,
Les jardins français,
dated 1821.

11.

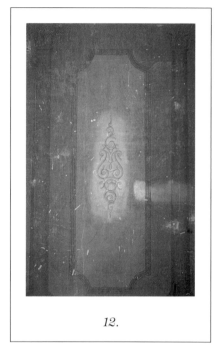

12.

No doubt similar work was done in houses in Atlantic Canada during the early 1800s, although the oldest extant stencilled wall decoration so far discovered in Nova Scotia in the Hillsdale House, Annapolis Royal, dates from after 1849 *(fig. 12)*.[28] More abundant in the Maritimes are painted rooms decorated free-hand, including figurative compositions, decorative borders, imitation woodgraining and marbleizing. The earliest figurative wall painting discovered in Nova Scotia, in the Lunenburg County Court House, is an oil on plaster mural of a British coat of arms perched on a pedestal which predates the Croscup paintings by some thirty-six years *(fig. 13)*.

The production of scenic wall paintings in North America demanded considerably more from the provincial painter-decorator in terms of technical skills, manual dexterity, artistic sensitivity, and imagination than simple stencil work, woodgraining, or marbleizing. Many professional and amateur decorators therefore turned for advice to one or other of the numerous British or American art instruction books and periodicals in general circulation in North America from the late eighteenth century. These provided information on various designs and methods of

11.
This stencilled overmantel, condition as found, was made for the Van Sickle House, Jerseyville, Ont., in about 1825.

12.
Interior of the Hillsdale House, Annapolis Royal, N.S., built about 1849 for Susan Foster as a hotel. Shown is a wall of the former dining room (since covered over), painted with a stencilled illusionary panel moulding, framing Corinthian columns, and a central freehand arabesque motif.

13.

14.

13.
On the first floor of the Court House (now the parish hall of St. John's church) at Lunenburg, N.S., is this oil on plaster mural of the British royal coat of arms, from 1801–14, depicted mounted on a pedestal. The mural is dated c. 1810.

14.
Murals painted about 1825 by Rufus Porter (1792–1884) for a house in Lyme, Grafton County, N.H.

ornamenting walls, floors, and woodwork, along with updates on the latest fashions. British horticulturalist and writer on architecture, John Claudius Loudon (1743–1843), for one, considerably influenced Canadian and American tastes in domestic architecture and interior design through his seminal book, *Encyclopædia of Cottage, Farm and Villa Architecture and Furniture*. First published in England in 1833, this publication was widely read by English, American, and Canadian architects, interior decorators, and homeowners, going through eleven reprints between 1834 and 1867 alone.

One of the best-selling books published in North America in the second quarter of the nineteenth century was by Rufus Porter, then the leading American painter of popular scenic murals. Porter travelled widely throughout New England producing numerous unique panoramic paintings in various interiors *(fig. 14)*. While evidently inspired by scenic wallpapers of the day, these were original in content and style. During the 1820s Porter perfected and promoted a fast and inexpensive method of painting scenic murals on plaster. His 1825 do-it-yourself manual, reprinted several times in 1826 as *A Select Collection of Valuable and Curious Arts and Interesting Experiments*, offered practical lessons in landscape painting on walls and various other types of decorative painting techniques. Extracts were later republished in serial form in the journals *New York Mechanic* (1841–42) and *Scientific American* (1845–46), of which Porter was founder and editor.[29]

In their scale, general design, and narrative nature, the Croscup murals resemble early nineteenth-century scenic wallpapers. Although each of the eleven paintings is treated as a distinct, self-contained pictorial unit rather than as part of an episodic story or panoramic sequence, an effort has been made to integrate them into a coherent ensemble. This heterogeneous group has been unified in three ways: by the continuous border of woodgrained trim skirting the floor, windows, and doors; by the ingenious linking of the panels by means of the red *trompe l'œil* curtain running along the upper edges; and by making certain formal adjustments to individual compositions so they better relate to neighbouring pictures and to their architectural setting.

Like many early architectural painters, the Croscup artist combined freehand figurative painting with purely ornamental work. The woodwork framing the murals has been both grained and marbleized – two common forms of "imitation" painting. According to Rufus Porter's 1846 account: "This branch [of painting] has probably never been so much in vogue as at present. Imitation or pretended imitations of oak, maple, mahogany, or marble, may be seen on three-fourths of the doors of houses in the cities [North American], besides wainscotting, chimney pieces and furniture."[30]

Graining was a common nineteenth-century technique whereby a more lowly wood, such as the pine found in most Nova Scotia homes, was made to appear as a finer species of wood. In the Croscup parlour the doors and door frames, window frames, sashes, and lower panels have been mottled, streaked, and pockmarked with an ochre wash over a straw-coloured ground to resemble what is most probably figured maple. The baseboard, on the other hand, is coloured a warm brown with a plumed reddish-brown painted grain no doubt meant to suggest a mahogany veneer. As exemplified in this interior, the intended visual effect, observed J.C. Loudon in 1833, was not "of having the imitation mistaken for the original, but rather to create an allusion to it, and by a diversity of lines to produce a kind of variety and intricacy which affords more pleasure to the eye than a flat shade of colour."[31] This allusive approach to imitating natural materials differed from the more scientific attitude of later Victorian painters who strove for a degree of realistic representation that perfectly fooled the eye. The Croscup artist adopts a similar formal attitude in his decoration of the parlour mantel.

The wooden Adam-style mantelpiece is painted to generally simulate a dark green mottled marble, probably of a species frequently referred to in the 1800s as "Egyptian" marble. To again quote Porter: "In imitating the Egyptian marble, the ground is painted nearly black, and the graining or clouding is formed with various lighter colours. In all attempts at imitation, the practitioner should be furnished with choice specimens of the real article, and imitate by sight and judgement, as no specific rules can possibly be given whereby he can succeed without a sample."[32] Whether or not the Croscup artist had access to an actual piece of the marble imitated or copied a printed illustration, he reveals in his marbleizing as in his graining an obvious technical command indicative of some training and practical experience.

The idea of framing each wall with painted red drapery caught up in swags with tasselled bows of gold cord on a black rod like a folded theatre curtain or window drapes was not original to the Croscup artist, though rendered here in a unique and effective manner. Framing pictorial drapery, often red, was a standard artistic convention in European painting well before the eighteenth century. This convention was taken up by early North American painters, notably in colonial portraiture, where drapery falling from one corner just before or behind the sitter served as an enhancing frame or a background foil *(fig. 15)*.[33] Windows, draped in a fashion similar to the Croscup *trompe l'œil* curtain and opening onto a landscape, may also be found in

15.

group or single portraits with interior settings produced by professional and amateur colonial artists. In like manner, portraits set outdoors often include heavy drapery screens between the foreground where the subjects stand and a rapidly receding panoramic landscape in the background.

Illusionistic curtains framing interior decorative wall paintings were evidently fashionable in North American homes before the Croscup room was painted, as seen in the overmantel painting from about 1825 in the Palmer house, Canterbury, Connecticut *(fig. 16)*. An awareness by the muralist of the pictorial conventions of easel painting in part explains the appearance of such painted border curtains in domestic decorative murals. Also to be considered is the influence of printed wallpapers on North American painter-decorators. Frieze or border papers, printed with draped curtain patterns rendered with varying degrees of realism, were popular in the late 1700s and

16.

16.
Overmantel, oil on wood,
painted about 1820 for a house
in Canterbury, Windham County,
Conn.

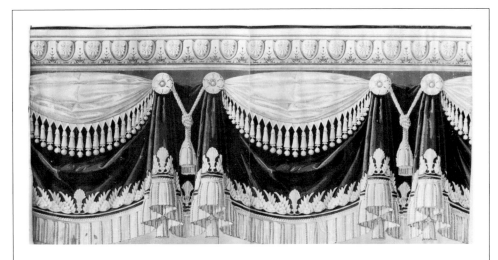

17.

18.

17.
French frieze wallpaper,
block print, dated c. 1810–15.
Collection: Union centrale des
arts décoratifs, Paris.

18.
A stencilled parlour wall from
the 1820s, condition as found,
in the Detta-Mouck House, South
Bay, Prince Edward County, Ont.
Collection: Canadian Museum of
Civilization.

19.
Front room of a house in Mabou
Mines, N.S., built about 1850.
The red tassel-fringed curtain
(now faded to brown) was
painted freehand on the wooden
walls along the ceiling edge.
Although simpler and more
naïvely rendered than the
drapery border in the Croscup
parlour, this curtain relates to
the Croscup artist's drapery in
that it is also conceived as a
continuous frieze encircling the
room. In this interior, however,
the curtain is a primary decorative
element, floating high above the
chair rail like a canopy over two
stylized trees of life on either
side of the mantelpiece.

19.

the 1800s *(fig. 17)*. Stylized swag-like hand stencilled decorative borders imitating wallpaper have been found on the walls of both Canadian and American interiors *(fig. 18)*. More representative freehand curtain motifs edging the wall at the ceiling, like a frieze, were also painted for provincial house interiors. A good example in Atlantic Canada is to be found in a front room of a house in Mabou Mines, Nova Scotia, painted about four to five years after the Croscup room *(fig. 19)*.[34]

The secondary ornamentation of the Croscup parlour, comprising the grained architectural trim, marbleized mantel, and painted curtain frames, is an important and inseparable part of the decorative ensemble, serving to enrich, define, and give finish to the interior as a whole. Yet while this ornamentation is rendered with notable skill and refinement compared with the known "fancy architectural" work of other provincial painter-decorators, ultimately it is the murals themselves that distinguish the Croscups' parlour from all other extant domestic interiors decorated in Canada before Confederation. Surviving examples of this type of scenic wall painting are extremely rare in

Canada although many have been located in New England homes.[35] Considering American domestic painted interiors as well, the work of the Croscup artist may be said to stand equal to the best examples of its day.

Probably academically untutored, the Croscup artist nonetheless exhibits a good understanding of design and of decorative techniques and materials. This was perhaps learned during training as an apprentice to another provincial – possibly British, if indeed he came from England – painter-decorator. He may also have learned his craft from reading books and articles, such as Porter's, and from practical experience. Analysis of the murals themselves reveals the hand of a distinctive artistic personality.

2

*The
Murals-
Victorian
Prospects*

HE CROSCUP MURALS feature a diverse range of subjects representing a fascinating cross section of contemporary life during the relatively short time span of the 1830s and early 1840s as seen from a colonial perspective. Not merely ornamental, they are also important social and historical documents of considerable artistic merit, evidently portraying subjects of some personal significance to William Croscup and his family. For today's visitor, as for art and social historians, these long-forgotten wall paintings provide insight into tastes and customs of the past, and at the same time offer a compelling aesthetic experience.

The paintings were executed in carbon pencil and oil on lime plaster keyed to wood lath attached to wall studs. The plaster, though of poor quality, was found during restoration to have been well applied, carefully smoothed, and apparently primed with glue size before being painted and then protected with a coat or more of varnish. The forms of the images were first outlined in carbon pencil then overpainted in a variety of bright oil colours ranging from an almost opaque to a diluted transparent consistency. Whereas some images appear hastily drawn and incomplete, others were given a greater definition and degree of finish through selective overdrawing in pencil and a diluted brown oil paint, thought to have been applied with a quill pen.[36]

There is a marked difference in the degree of formal sophistication and finish between, as well as within, the individual pictures. These stylistic discrepancies, not readily explainable, have naturally led to speculation about the identity of the artist. In a seminal 1982 article examining the iconography of the Croscup murals, Gilbert Gignac and Jeanne L'Espérance theorized that, despite family lore, "it might in fact have been a local inhabitant and possibly even a woman who painted the walls of the Croscup room." They also contemplate "the possibility that more than one hand was involved."[37] Given the quasi-mythical nature of much oral tradition, it is reasonable to question family belief that the Croscup painter was a down-on-his-luck Englishman, maybe a professional ship's painter, briefly exiled from his native land. While no extant North American paintings by the same hand have been discovered, early nineteenth-century commercial advertisements in Nova Scotia newspapers do mention several ornamental house and ship's painters practising their profession locally who conceivably could have produced such murals, if sufficiently gifted and inspired.

The possibility of the artist, or an apprentice, being "a woman who lived in the Croscup house" seems, however, extremely remote, despite the tenacious argument advanced in the Gignac-L'Espérance paper.[38] Although other instances of women amateurs trying their hand at interior decorative painting have been documented,[39] the fact is that Hannah Croscup was the only woman in the Croscup family known to have been living in the Karsdale house before 1850 and she is a highly improbable candidate for the artist.[40] In any event, some credence should be given to the basic facts of family tradition – that the artist was a man and, quite possibly, English born.

A more plausible explanation for formal inconsistencies in the murals, it is felt, may be found in the different visual sources employed in composing the pictures. It has been established by Gignac and L'Espérance that several of the images derive from popular prints, specifically from fashion plates and from wood engravings of contemporary subjects published in early issues of *The Illustrated London News*, the first English-language illustrated newspaper in the nineteenth century which, from its launching in May 1842, had a wide circulation throughout North America. When working from a visual model such as a print, the artist was able to reproduce his chosen subject with greater veracity than when he depended on memory alone. It seems unlikely that the Croscup artist produced any of the wall paintings from sketches made directly from nature. He appears to have depended more on memory in combination with secondary illustrations, thereby creating images that vary in degree of realism and formal accomplishment. This approach to artistic creation allowed for a personal, albeit eclectic, interpretation of chosen subjects. Our understanding of the pictorial significance of the Croscup murals, although still incomplete, has been greatly enhanced by the discovery of many of the design sources for the images. This has helped shed light on the artist's working methods, certain artistic influences, and some of his main aesthetic concerns.

Plate 1

Parlour, west wall, Croscup-Hall House
Karsdale, Nova Scotia, c. 1846–48
Oil and carbon pencil on plaster
236 × 459 cm

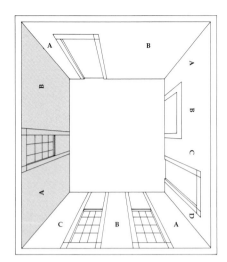

PANEL A

Trafalgar Square, London

Based on a wood engraving in *The Illustrated London News* (fig. 19), this view is drawn from the west side of Trafalgar Square, looking along the façade of the National Gallery toward the Church of St. Martin-in-the-Fields. Generally faithful to actual appearances, the artist nonetheless chose to fill the square with water to complement the adjoining panel depicting the Neva River and Peter 1 Square, Saint Petersburg. The foreground studies of people and carriages in the engraved model were evidently of little direct interest to the Croscup artist compared with the urban setting proper. Only two of the carriages and a small number of the figures, all rather loosely and sometimes incompletely rendered, have been retained.

PANEL B

Peter 1 Square, Saint Petersburg, Russia

As in panel A, this view is also based on a wood engraving in *The Illustrated London News* (fig. 20). The prospect is southward across the Neva River bridge toward St. Isaac's Cathedral, flanked on the right by the Manège (riding school) of the Horse Guards, the long façade of the Senate Building and, nearest the viewer, the Holy Synod Building. The representation in the engraving of the great military review and crowds of spectators connected with the meeting of the Russian and Prussian heads of state – the primary subject of the print – have been replaced in this panel by a new composition of strolling, riding, and otherwise delightfully interactive figures evidently of the Croscup artist's own invention. Note the two boxers and attendant referees involved in a bout of fisticuffs before the cathedral and the group of brightly attired figures in the lower right corner. This party of two women and three top-hatted men in fashionable mid-1830s street clothes appear by their poses and gestures to be somehow personally related. There is a striking resemblance in pose and dress of the central female figure, with the long blue scarf and green robe, to that of the bonnetted woman, far right, in panel C of the east wall (*pl. 3*). Both look outward toward the spectator in a familiar manner, suggesting they may represent specific individuals acquainted or related to the Croscups. As the Annapolis Valley was home to a significant number of black settlers, perhaps the two black men to the left of this group depict Nova Scotians. Or perhaps they are just imaginary representations of the variety of people to be found in a bustling international port of call.

Plate 2

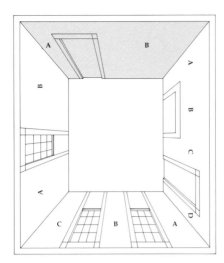

Parlour, north wall, Croscup-Hall House
Karsdale, Nova Scotia, c. 1846–48
Oil and carbon pencil on plaster
236 × 394 cm

PANEL A

Decorative Landscape

PANEL B

*Atlantic Harbour Scene
with Ship Launching*

Maritime views were among
the favoured subjects that early
provincial painter-decorators were
asked to produce for domestic
interiors, as many of their patrons,
like William Croscup, were in
some way connected with maritime commerce and lived near a
port or major waterway. This
dynamic port scene, centred
around a ship launching, conveys
a sense of the varied activities of a
prosperous northeastern Atlantic
community. In some aspects it
recalls the Annapolis Royal
harbour district, in others, Halifax.
The subject may in fact be imaginary, generally evoking rather
than documenting the social and
commercial realities of maritime
life in Nova Scotia of the 1840s.

Plate 3

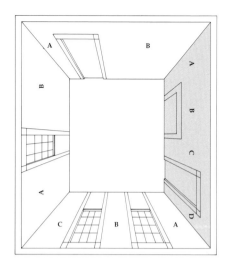

Parlour, east wall, Croscup-Hall House
Karsdale, Nova Scotia, c. 1846–48
Oil and carbon pencil on plaster
236 × 456 cm

PANEL A

Mother and Child

Croscup family tradition identifies the figures as Hannah Amelia Croscup and her first daughter, Lucretia, born on 8 February 1846. The style of dress of the mother and child and the surrounding vegetation support the belief that this panel probably represents a local subject. The woman's wide-skirted dress with leg-of-mutton sleeves and her muslin ruffled house cap were worn in Canada from the early 1830s into the 1840s, though no longer the height of fashion by 1835.

PANEL B

Queen Victoria and Prince Albert Presenting Princess Victoria, Prince Edward, and Princess Alice to Louis-Philippe, King of the French

The practice of decorating domestic interiors with images of reigning sovereigns was fairly common in English homes, more so following the coronation of Queen Victoria on 20 June 1837. The stature and popularity of the British monarchy increased greatly during Victoria's reign. The Queen's youth, successful marriage in 1840 to Prince Albert, and early motherhood – by 1845 there were four children – were major reasons for the public's favourable attitude. Some of the Queen's staunchest fans were Nova Scotians, many with Loyalist backgrounds, who could recall that Victoria's father, the Duke of Kent, served as Lieutenant-General in Halifax during the 1790s.

PANEL C

Scottish Piper and Three Ladies in a Rural Setting

This enigmatic picture evokes the pleasures of rural society. Similar in general composition to panel A, it depicts four large figures out-doors on an earthen road or clearing that appears to be a continuation of the path under the feet of the mother and child. The forms of the trees in panel A are echoed in the voluminous rosebush and the row of tall trees behind the piper and ladies. The two panels thereby complement each other and visually balance the fireplace wall.

PANEL D

Decorative Landscape

Plate 4

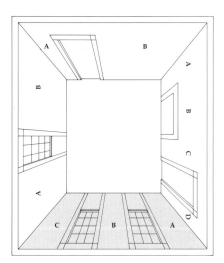

Parlour, south wall, Croscup-Hall House,
Karsdale, Nova Scotia, c. 1846–48
Oil and carbon pencil on plaster,
236 × 394 cm

PANEL A

Mimac Family

This original composition pictures
a young Micmac mother seated on
a rock by a shore, one child at her
knee, another peering out from a
distant wigwam. A male figure,
presumably the father of the family, stands nearby. The colourful
costumes and unique possessions
identify the figures as members of
the Micmac tribe. The woman is
traditionally attired in a long dark
dress with fitted leggings, an
embroidered beige blanket-shawl,
and an indigo red braid-trimmed
peaked hat of typical Micmac
design. The man wears a red-
piped, blue frock-type coat
clinched at the waist by a leather
belt. On his head is a top hat with
a clay pipe in the hatband, a popular part of mid-nineteenth century Micmac dress. The woman's
quill basket, the wigwams – their
birchbark covering simply described
in a block-like pattern of brown
lines – and the bark canoe are also
of distinctive Micmac manufacture.
The canoe has been dramatically
cropped by the artist at the far left
corner of the panel rather than
being carried over onto the east
wall.

PANEL B

Hunter

A popular print of Prince Albert
buck shooting in the Scottish
highlands (fig. 42) evidently was
the prototype for this image of a
gentleman hunter and his deer-
hound in a forest clearing. The
resemblance of the background
greenery to that in panel A
suggests, however, that it was
meant to represent a local Nova
Scotian. Any specific visual
references to the royal personnage
have been avoided.

PANEL C

Landscape with Waterfall

As in panels A and C on the east
wall (pl. 3), the artist attempts
to unify the three south panels
through background landscape.
If not continuous, the panels do
portray a similar range of native
coniferous and deciduous trees
whose forms echo each other.

WEST WALL: FOREIGN ENCOUNTERS

The main entrance to the Croscup parlour was situated just to the left of the front hall on the east wall of the room *(pl. 2)*. Passing through this doorway, the visitor first confronted the west wall, divided by a window located just left of centre into two large panels of equal height but slightly varied width *(pl. 1)*. The artist chose to fill these spaces with a pair of monumental urban views, serving at once to balance and help unify the divided wall as well as to impress the visitor on entering the room. On the left is Trafalgar Square in London, England, and on the right, Peter I Square in Saint Petersburg, Russia (today known as Dekabrist Square, Leningrad).

In creating these murals the Croscup artist evidently had access to wood engravings from *The Illustrated London News* which served as his primary models. The London view is based on the engraving "Trafalgar Square" reproduced in the issue of 10 September 1842 *(fig. 20)*.[41] The view of Saint Petersburg was drawn after the engraving on the front page of the 27 August 1842 edition, which depicted the ceremonial public meeting of the Emperor of Russia and the King of Prussia *(fig. 21)*.[42] These views were obviously selected and rendered as companion pieces. Although different in content, they represent similar subjects which complement each other almost perfectly and encourage us to read each panel as part of an integrated pictorial unit encompassing the whole western wall.

The Croscup artist's painting of Trafalgar Square, as in the published engraving, depicts the English landmark from the west, looking across the square along the south façade of the National Gallery built in 1838 and further eastward down the public walkway to the Church of St. Martin-in-the-Fields (rebuilt by James Gibb in 1721–26). Equally faithful to its printed source in terms of its vantage point and principal subjects, the Saint Petersburg panel represents a view from the north bank of the Neva River looking south over the bridge toward St. Isaac's Cathedral. To the west (the viewer's right) of the church is a row of smaller, near-identical state buildings, punctuated by the Manège, or riding school, of the Horse Guards with its distinctive triangular pediment and colonnade. Spanning the west side of Peter I Square, from the middle to the foreground, stands the massive

20.
"Trafalgar Square," wood engraving in *The Illustrated London News*, 10 September 1842. Collection: National Library of Canada.

21.
"Meeting of the Emperor of Russia and King of Prussia at Saint Petersburg," wood engraving in *The Illustrated London News*, 27 August 1842. This site in the heart of Saint Petersburg was the object of much attention even without that engendered by momentous events such as the meeting of national rulers. Between 1818 and 1857, St. Isaac's Cathedral – a monumental project – was being planned and built. French-born designer Richard Auguste de Montferrand did his own share to publicize both his project and Peter I Square in his book, published in 1845. Near completion by 1841, St. Isaac's and the recently completed Senate and Holy Synod buildings made Peter I Square the main intersection and ceremonial focus of the city. Collection: National Library of Canada.

20.

21.

Senate Building which connects almost imperceptibly with that of the Holy Synod in the near right corner.

The buildings in both murals are similarly composed along strong diagonal lines extending from the lower outside corners toward a common horizon about mid-way up the parlour window frame and highlighted by a church. The opposing movement of these two lines of perspective creates a mirror-like effect. Seen together, the murals create the illusion of forms mutually receding into space toward an imaginary vanishing point situated somewhere outside the parlour window.

By referring to a print as his model, the Croscup artist was able to position and describe the buildings, figures, and accessory elements within each picture with greater accuracy than his somewhat limited skills as an architectural painter-decorator would permit. This working method also helped create the illusion of a deep, recessed space – a difficult task for the academically untrained painter. Through the example of the newspaper illustrators (who here remain nameless) the Croscup artist was introduced to the tradition of perspective urban view painting. Rooted stylistically in the eighteenth-century townscapes of Venetian painter Canaletto (1697–1768) and his followers, this pictorial tradition was developed through the late 1700s and early 1800s by British topographic artists, among others.

Perspective views of town squares, along with urban panoramas and street scenes, were much admired and in demand from the late eighteenth through the early nineteenth centuries in North America as well as in Britain where popular prints after original studies of urban subjects circulated widely. Richard Short (active from 1759 to 1761), Robert A. Sproule (1799–1845), James Pattison Cockburn (1779–1847), John Elliot Woolford (1778–1866), and George Heriot (1766–1844) are just a few of the British-born topographic painters active in Canada before 1850 who made drawings and paintings of Canadian townscapes, some of which were made into prints, that conform to the basic formula of perspective view painting. The drawing of *Place d'Armes Montreal* by John Murray (born in 1810, died after 1868), engraved and published about 1843–44 by Adolphus Bourne (active from 1820 to 1880), is representative of this type *(fig. 22)*. Almost contemporary with the engravings of Trafalgar Square and Saint Petersburg in *The Illustrated London News*, "reinterpre-

22.

Place d'Armes, Montreal, drawn by John Murray, engraved by [A] Bourne, published in Montreal about 1843–44. The viewpoint here, as in *figs. 19* and *20*, is defined by the careful delineation of buildings around the square. With near mathematical precision the buildings on the left recede in a strong diagonal sweep toward the focus of the picture – the church. The architecture here is of primary interest, but human figures, representing facets of contemporary society, animate the otherwise static stage-like scene, introducing the main subject – the city – and providing a measure of scale. Collection: Royal Ontario Museum, Toronto (940x66.3).

22.

ted" on the west wall of the Croscups' parlour, it is a good comparative example. The formal and conceptual similarities between the Canadian and European views of these famous landmarks, especially that of Trafalgar Square, reflect their common stylistic roots rather than direct influences.

Evidently it was the permanent aspects of Trafalgar and Peter I Squares, as portrayed in *The Illustrated London News*, more than the variable details of contemporary life in the diverse groups of figures in the foreground that appealed to the Croscup artist and, by extension, the Croscup family. In an effort to ensure that the painted versions of these urban subjects remained identifiable, the Croscup artist was quite faithful in reproducing the composition and the salient architectural forms. Yet, while concerned with achieving a reasonable likeness, he evidently felt no need to transcribe his subjects in exacting detail. The murals may best be described as "adaptations" or "creative reproductions" rather than as copies of the prints.

The Croscup artist's background as a decorator is evident in the preoccupation with problems of design that at times override descriptive concerns. In an effort to create a more pleasing, unified design, he is willing to alter the appearance of an object or setting. For example, in the view of Trafalgar Square, the plain retaining wall running around the outside of the public walkway as depicted in the published engraving has been transformed into an arched balustrade identical to the inner one. Even more striking is the transformation of the paved inner court of Trafalgar Square into a pool of water, an act understandable only when seen in light of the flanking Saint Petersburg panel which features the Neva River. So, too – perhaps due to difficulties reading details in the small prints as well as concern with clarifying vague passages that would stand out when enlarged onto the wall – the artist redesigned the façade windows of both the National Gallery and the Church of St. Martin-in-the-Fields in the areas behind the entrance porticos. In the engraving, these areas are obscured by darkly hatched shadows.

In the transformation of the prints into wall paintings, the images undergo a general process of simplification: objects are reduced to essential forms and certain omissions are made. This formal reductionism may only partly be explained in terms of artistic emphasis on the permanent over the temporary aspects of the subjects. For how can one explain the Croscup artist's omitting certain telling features seen in the prints, such as the distinctive Royal Arms on the pediment and the circular tower windows in the Church of St. Martin-in-the-Fields in Trafalgar Square, or the renowned equestrian statue of Peter the Great in Peter I Square? One again suspects that problems related to the articulation on a large scale of vaguely defined objects in the prints to be a factor. Not to be overlooked, however, are the artist's own intentions, not to mention the limitations of his painterly skills. By removing the formally complex monument to Peter the Great, for example, an unobstructed view toward St. Isaac's Cathedral is maintained in accordance with the composition of the flanking view of Trafalgar Square.

As sites of major nineteenth-century architectural projects, Trafalgar Square, with the initially controversial new National

Gallery building, and its Saint Petersburg counterpart drew attention as prime examples of the latest achievements in urban planning and redevelopment. Although not uncriticized, they nonetheless became international symbols of social, cultural, and technological progress in Europe. For the youthful William and Hannah Croscup, whose role in selecting the pictures to adorn their home must have equalled, if not occasionally supplanted, the artist's, the very modernity of the subjects – inspired by illustrations from one of the most progressive periodicals of the time – may have significantly contributed to their appeal. Indeed, an interest in the people, places, and events of contemporary life, expressed throughout the Croscup parlour, is one of the points of distinction in this group of wall paintings.

The absence of documentation makes it impossible to unequivocally establish the precise meaning and full personal significance of the mural subjects to the artist and the Croscups. Much, however, can be surmised. If not conceived as episodes in some unfolding panorama or drama, the pictures do reveal thematic affiliations linking them iconographically.

The commanding presence of a pair of foreign cityscapes on their parlour wall may be seen as an expression of the cosmopolitan outlook of the Croscups, a cosmopolitanism shaped by their involvement, like many of their Nova Scotian neighbours, in the international shipping and timber trades. London and Saint Petersburg were not only the political capitals of two major European powers but also the leading trade and distribution centres of the timber industry, in which Nova Scotia had become an important participant from the time of the French continental blockade during the Napoleonic Wars. In fact, English Quay in Saint Petersburg, where Balkan wood products were traded to English shipping merchants, was just a short distance from Peter I Square down the Neva River embankment.[43] The commercial significance of these trade centres was probably not without special meaning for a shipbuilder such as William Croscup. The view of Trafalgar Square, a central landmark at the very heart of the British Empire, may have had personal as well as commercial and cultural meaning for the Croscups in light of their Loyalist background. In this respect, the Trafalgar Square panel may also be seen to relate thematically to the picture of the British royal family on the east wall.

EAST WALL: DOMESTIC VIRTUES

Compared with the simple, bipartite division of the west wall, the east wall is decorated with three relatively small murals organized around the fireplace, with a fourth panel running down the right side of the main entrance *(pl. 3)*. Featured above the marbleized mantelpiece is a painting of Queen Victoria and Prince Albert presenting the royal children to King Louis-Philippe of France. The painted architectural frame around this picture, which echoes the form of stucco overmantels, gives the illusion of extending the mantelpiece to the ceiling and thus effectively both highlights and separates the central image from the flanking views of a mother and child (left) and a Scottish piper and ladies (right).

A familiar picture of the British royal household typifying the joys of family life seems an apt icon to occupy the honoured position above the Croscup hearth. The Queen was not only a symbol of the State, she was also a social role model. The happy home life of the British royal family was viewed in the mid-nineteenth century as the epitome of domestic virtue and contentment; indeed, the Queen was revered, to quote from *Godey's Lady's Book* of February 1844, as "the *good mother* we consider the most exalted character which humanity affords."[44] Interest and admiration for British royalty at this time is reflected in the proliferation of pictures of its members in the 1840s, ranging from formal portraits and conversation pieces by court artists Edwin Landseer (1802–1873) and Franz Xavier Winterhalter (1805–1873) to popular prints and illustrations connected with accounts of the Queen's life and activities found, for example, in *The Illustrated London News*.

The Croscup overmantel painting is, in fact, partly derived from a wood engraving entitled "The Crimson Drawing Room – Introduction of Louis-Philippe to the Infant Royal Family," appearing in the 12 October 1844 issue of *The Illustrated London News (fig. 23)*.[45] Like the print, the painting represents an intimate gathering of the royal family with the "King of the French" during his visit to England in October 1844. This visit had been organized essentially as a private social call by the French head of state to reciprocate the hospitality extended to Queen Victoria and Prince Albert during their sojourn in France the previous

23.

23.
"Visit of the King of the French to Queen Victoria: The Crimson Drawing Room – Introduction of Louis-Philippe to the Infant Royal Family," wood engraving in *The Illustrated London News*, 12 October 1844. Collection: National Library of Canada.

summer. Although the Queen emphasized its informality, this brief visit had considerable historical and political significance as it was the first by a reigning French sovereign to England since 1356. It therefore generated much interest among British subjects who were kept informed about the royal itinerary through the press. Nova Scotians were notified of Louis-Philippe's impending trip to England as early as 19 August 1844 in *The Nova Scotian*, which closely followed the sometimes controversial tour in subsequent issues.[46]

Relations between the French and British royal families at this time were close, enhanced by personal ties that went beyond political considerations. Accompanied by his youngest son, Antoine, the Duc de Montpensier, and a large political delegation, the 71-year-old Louis-Philippe spent the week of 8 October 1844 as the young Queen's guest. Upon arriving in England, Louis-Philippe was received by the Queen and her entourage in the state apartments at Windsor Castle. A formal dinner reception attended by thirty dignitaries, including the Duke of Wellington and British Prime Minister Sir Robert Peel, was held that evening in the Queen's private dining room. It was following this reception that the King was introduced to the Queen's two eldest children, Victoria, the Princess Royal, then aged four, and

24.

25.

24.

Présentation des enfants de la reine Victoria au roi des Français, 1844, by Édouard-Henri Théophile Pingret. Watercolour and graphite on paper. In Pingret's version of this event, the meeting of Louis-Philippe with the British royal children is shown as occurring in one of the chandeliered reception rooms at Windsor Castle. Surrounded by a large entourage, the Queen stands at the centre presenting Victoria, the Princess Royal, and Prince Edward, who move toward the French sovereign. Collection: Musée du Louvre, Paris.

25.

La reine Victoria reçoit le roi Louis-Philippe au château de Windsor, 1844, by Franz-Xavier Winterhalter. Oil on canvas, 345 × 480 cm. Winterhalter's picture is more formal than Pingret's *(fig. 23)*, accenting the ceremonial nature of the meeting of British and French royalty, with the children accorded a secondary role. The artist has added the figure of the youngest of the British royal children, Princess Alice, who did not actually meet Louis-Philippe. Collection: Musée national du château de Versailles, Versailles.

26.

Louis-Philippe 1er, roi des français, et Victoria 1re, reine d'Angleterre au château de Windsor, le 9 octobre 1844, by Jean Alaux. Charcoal, pencil, white gouache, brown wash heightened with red and yellow on paper, 48.6 × 64.5 cm. Collection: Musée de Besançon, Besançon, France.

26.

three-year-old Prince Edward (later King Edward VII). Édouard Pingret (1788–1875), Franz Xavier Winterhalter (1805–1873), Louis Haghe (1806–1885), and Joseph Nash (1808–1878) were among the international group of painters engaged to record this and other events of the visit.[47]

Deviating from the official commemorative paintings of Pingret and Winterhalter *(figs. 24, 25)* which, closer to reality, depict the introduction of the Queen's children as a public affair taking place in one of the great reception halls of Windsor Castle, *The Illustrated London News* version of this event situates it in a secluded corner of the "crimson or principal drawing room." Pictorial interest here focusses on the private, even playful, nature of this royal gathering, which includes, albeit inaccurately, the Queen's youngest child, one-year-old Princess Alice. This interpretation conforms more nearly to the intended, if not actual, character of the French King's trip to England. As repeated in the related newspaper article, it was the wish of Her Majesty, as well as that of Louis-Philippe, "…to treat this visit as one of a private nature…." The crowd of spectators is reduced to a small peripheral group of seven figures standing behind the sofa on which the King and Queen sit. The simple composition and intimate tone of the magazine illustration relates more to the small life studies of the English and French heads of state produced by Jean Alaux (1786–1864), one of which is remarkably similar *(fig. 26)*.

The Croscup artist's own interpretation of this scene combines the intimate with the grand. In so doing, the overmantel painting emphasizes both the public and private lives of royalty seen at once as heads of state and as caring human beings. Reproducing the principal figures from the engraving, he relocates them within the more magnificent context of a richly decorated vaulted room akin in design to the great public spaces in Windsor Castle. As in the west wall murals, details of the print are freely changed in accordance with the artist's personal aesthetic concerns, yet not to a point where the subject is no longer identifiable. The forms and poses in the print of the King and Queen on the sofa, Prince Albert and the three royal children in the centre of the room, and five of the courtiers behind the sofa have all been transferred onto the wall of the Croscup room with a reasonable degree of fidelity. More attention is paid, however, to the decorative aspect of the image, apparent in the room

27.

28.

27.
"Visit of the King of the French to Queen Victoria: The Grand Corridor – The Queen and the Royal Visitors Passing to the Banquet," wood engraving, by S. Sly, in *The Illustrated London News*, 12 October 1844. This print may have inspired the design of the windows, curtains, and ceiling coffers of the room portrayed in the Croscup overmantel painting. Collection: National Library of Canada.

28.
"Visit of the King of the French to Queen Victoria: Grand Staircase, Windsor Castle – Her Majesty Receiving Her Royal Guests," wood engraving in *The Illustrated London News*, 12 October 1844. The imperial crown and lions decorating the white marbleized arch in the Croscup overmantel evidently are based on elements from the royal insignia embellishing the magazine article about Louis-Philippe's English tour. The lions in the Croscup mural closely follow the form of the lion in the engraving, with the one in the left corner of the mural rendered in reverse to balance the design. Collection: National Library of Canada.

decor, with its boldly patterned carpet and coffered ceiling, and in the colourful embellishment of the costumes and accessories.

The room and the frame enclosing the figures are largely the product of the Croscup artist's own imagination (*figs. 27, 28*). By repeating the forms of the two Doric columns in the foreground and extending the archway over them in progressively diminishing size toward the painted back wall, the artist created an effective, if limited and spatially ambiguous, stage set for the figures. Formally, this mural exhibits some of the same technical problems and design concerns that frequently typify the work of many non-academic painters. For example, the figures are too large in relation to their environment. They do not fit comfortably into their allotted spaces, most obvious in the awkwardly placed figures cramped between the couch and the right wall of the room. The floor also tilts forward at a steep angle, somewhat at odds with the definition and placement of the sofa, the foreground figures, and the architecture, which attempt to create a sense of three-dimensional, receding space. The boldly patterned carpet further accents the two-dimensionality of the image.

In the narrow spaces on either side of the fireplace, and balancing the interior setting of the overmantel picture, are two complementary scenes depicting figures in a landscape. The mural to the left, representing a young mother holding her infant child up to the viewer, reiterates the theme of family expressed in the picture of Queen Victoria and Prince Albert with their children. The appeal of this maternal scene is, however, more direct. The much larger, frontally posed mother and child engage the eye of the spectator as they stare outward with more directness and naturalness than do the figures of royalty, whose absorption in their own activities tends to exclude the onlooker.

It has been said by a family descendant that this panel is meant to represent Hannah Amelia Croscup and her daughter, Lucretia, born on 8 February 1846.[48] The candour of the poses and expressions does seem to hint at an underlying personality beneath the schematized forms. This and the fact that these are the largest figures in the room gives them a special status which would support such an opinion, despite the lack of formal individualization of the subjects. If one accepts the family's identification, along with oral tradition claiming that the room was

29.

30.

painted over one winter, one could tentatively suggest as narrow a production date for the murals as between late 1846 and early 1847.[49] Considering the topical nature of most of the wall paintings it seems fair to say that the Croscup murals probably do not postdate February 1848, when Louis-Philippe, portrayed over the mantel, abdicated. Admittedly, without solid documentation, even this dating remains a matter of conjecture.

On the right side of the hearth, complementing the maternal scene on the left, the artist painted an enigmatic picture of a Scottish piper and three young women outdoors on the grounds of some country estate. Like the overmantel panel this image combines borrowed and imaginary elements. The figures of the three women were quite likely inspired by popular fashion plates, specifically from the October 1833 issue of *Townsend's Monthly Selection of Parisian Costume*, one of several fashion magazines reaching North American homes in the mid-nineteenth century (*figs. 29–31*).[50] The Croscup artist makes certain modifications from the prints in the women's dresses and fashion accessories, changing details and adding colour. These are essentially cosmetic, except for the central figure in the mural, which is deliberately transformed from the bride in the print outfitted in a "bridal dress of India muslin" into just another elegantly gowned lady by the simple substitution of a black apron with white lace

29–31.
Fashion plates 523, 524, and 521 respectively, hand-coloured engravings in *Townsend's Monthly Selection of Parisian Costume*, October 1833.

29. Despite alterations to their costumes, the two women on the right behind the Scottish piper in the Croscup panel are readily identifiable with the two models to the far right in this popular fashion plate.

30. The silk, tulle-trimmed pelisse of the model at lower left is the prototype for the day dress worn by the woman to the far left, partially hidden by the piper, in the Croscup mural.

31.

32.

31. The similarity of the head and coiffure of the model at lower left to that of the woman, far left, in the mural suggest this – or a similar fashion illustration – was the source for the Croscup artist's design.
Collection: Thomas J. Watson Library, The Metropolitan Museum of Art, New York.

32.
"Dalkeith – The Duke of Buccleuch's," wood engraving, by S. Sly, in *The Illustrated London News*, 3 September 1842.
Collection: National Library of Canada.

trim for the all-white lace lap pieces down the front of the skirt. If not obviously a wedding party, who – and where – are the people in this panel? The two-storey building with Ionic columns in the background may represent a Nova Scotia residence, possibly seen by the artist in the Annapolis Valley where outstanding examples of early nineteenth-century architecture in the Greek Revival style could then be found.[51] Could the people be participants in some family or community festivity, where a Scottish piper would not be an unusual form of entertainment? Though the piper's costume is not accurately rendered, he is readily identified as a Highlander. Neatly fitted into the limited foreground space of the vertical composition, the seated piper – in fact impossibly posed for playing – works well formally by creating variety within the picture while establishing a visual link with the overmantel panel and its seated figures.

It has been suggested that the idea for this picture could have come from an engraved vignette of the Duke of Buccleuch's Scottish estate "Dalkeith" in *The Illustrated London News* of 3 September 1842 *(fig. 32)*.[52] Knowing the Croscup artist's use of other illustrations from the magazine, it is tempting to suppose that he may again have looked to it for inspiration. If so, it is in a more indirect way. The arcadian vision of the elegantly attired members of Scottish society lounging on the sprawling grounds of

Dalkeith is similar in spirit to the evocation of rural life painted next to the Croscup's hearth. Yet, except for the basic idea of well-dressed figures standing outdoors near a rather grand neo-classical building, the composition is quite different. The emblematic Highland piper of the published print, if serving at all as a model (some telling aspects of his uniform do appear on the Croscup piper) is completely transformed from a marginal figure to one of central importance in the pictorial narrative, the significance of which remains unclear.

Completing the east wall decorations is a narrow landscape squeezed between the main entrance and the south wall. Simply composed, it features a river flowing past an uninhabited forest of freely invented, stylized trees. It is evidently a decorative filler to unify the east and south walls. The small section of sky extends over the door frame to blend with the sky in the panel of the Scottish piper and ladies, while the river appears to turn the corner onto the south wall to merge with the water in the foreground of the forest scene with the Micmac family.

NORTH WALL: MARITIME ENTERPRISE

The Croscup artist's skills as a designer are apparent in his ability to identify and resolve the problems posed by the architecture of the room in the interest of a rational and harmonious decorative scheme. On the north wall, because of the off-centre location of the doorway, the space to be decorated was divided into a narrow panel on the left and an exceptionally large one on the right *(pl. 2)*. Here the artist boldly took advantage of the generous space available to him to produce a panoramic harbour scene focussing on a ship launching. This dynamic visual statement about life in Atlantic Canada formally and thematically balances the monumental foreign cityscapes on the adjoining west wall. A landscape painted on the left side of the door is linked with this maritime scene by a common sky extending over the doorway and by the forms of the framing trees and a small wooden house, which echo those of the thicket of trees and the warehouses in the right-hand panel.

Maritime views were among the favoured subjects that early provincial decorators were requested to illustrate in domestic interiors, for the good reason that their patrons along the Atlantic seaboard were usually involved in some way with maritime commerce or at the very least lived near a port or major waterway. The Croscup family, like many Nova Scotian families, lived in close association with the sea. William Croscup's own activities included the operation of a small shipyard beside his Karsdale home, with a slipway along the waterfront of his property.

The shipping and shipbuilding industries in Atlantic Canada enjoyed a period of unprecedented growth during the first decades of the nineteenth century, stimulated by a growing demand for regional staple goods – above all, timber. After the French continental blockade during the later years of the Napoleonic Wars threatened to cut off Britain's timber supply from the Baltic, British North America was looked to as an alternative supplier of wood products. The economy of the Atlantic colonies was based on the export of its natural resources, including fish, agricultural produce, and minerals, in addition to timber. As international demand for its unprocessed wares grew, the need for vessels to export staples, import manufactured goods, and ferry items to and from Atlantic ports and major trade centres increased, thereby stimulating the local shipping and shipbuilding industries.

Before 1850, Atlantic shipbuilders and owners tended to be individuals or family firms, like the Croscups, rather than joint-stock companies. Most of those involved with shipbuilding were regional residents committed to the development and improvement of their home communities. The involvement of most with shipping and shipbuilding evolved out of their activities with one or the other of the local resource-based businesses. Few were solely shipbuilders; like William Croscup they usually plied some other trade as well. William Croscup's own activities as a shipbuilder and investor probably evolved out of his concerns as a farmer to move his produce to local and foreign markets. His evident success in this area owed much to the healthy Atlantic economy and international demand.[53]

As noted by contemporary historians Eric W. Sager and Lewis R. Fisher, "Shipping was ... essential to the staple-based economies of Atlantic Canada. Because vessels were so important to the economy, they became part of the way of life, and part even of the culture, of coastal peoples. Sailing vessels became sources of civic pride and symbols of progress, and a harbour filled with sails was a sign of healthy trade and prosperity."[54] It is in this context that the Croscup artist's Atlantic harbour scene may be understood.

A ship launching was an important event in nineteenth-century Atlantic Canada, often a festive occasion attracting throngs of onlookers who would come to admire the results of months of work and to witness, not without some apprehension, the first major test of a vessel's seaworthiness. In the north mural, the artist recreates the activities surrounding such an event. Here we see a typical harbour scene introduced by a forested stretch of shore, featuring an A-frame building and a trio of boys fishing off a small wooden dock. In the left foreground is a seemingly incongruous image of two horses mounted by jockeys in colourful riding silks racing along a sandy coastal road. A group of cursorily-drawn spectators may be seen lining up along the far wharf and on the deck of the ship being launched. Other figures, simply rendered as dark silhouettes, look on from aboard a paddle-steamer pulling in from the right for a better view, while still more onlookers gather along the portside of a steam tugboat towing a full-rigged ship in the middleground. The swirling waves at the stern of the ship being launched suggest that the launch master has just knocked out the wedge supports and the vessel is sliding down the ways. The lively action is emphasized by the zigzag movement of land and water receding toward the horizon and by the varied shapes and placement of the boats. The two racing steeds heading in the opposite direction to the ship being launched further increase the sense of action and excited activity.

The symbolic aspect of this view, as emblematic of regional progress and civic pride, is underscored by the artist's mode of representation. Though generally conceived in realistic terms, the scene is an amalgam of borrowed and imaginary elements rather than a direct nature study. The Croscup artist has made every effort to convey the character and ambience of a particular town or region, so it is difficult to believe that the paintings do not represent a specific locale. Yet, despite the amount of descriptive detail and points of physical resemblance the picture appears

33.
Overmantel, oil on wood, from about 1825, possibly an imaginary view of Charlestown, Mass., before the American Revolution. Now installed in "Beauport," the Sleeper-McCann House, in Gloucester, Mass. Collection: Society for the Preservation of New England Antiquities, Boston.

33.

to be essentially an imaginative construct. Historical precedents for this approach can be found in North American decorative folk art, exemplified by an overmantel painting from a house in Marblehead, Massachusetts *(fig. 33)*, as well as in academic painting, for example the *veduta ideata*, or imaginary landscape, of Canaletto.

The landscape topography in the painting resembles to some extent that of Annapolis Royal and vicinity as seen from the east

34.

35.

looking down the Basin toward Digby Gut *(figs. 34, 35)* – an appropriate scene to adorn the Croscups' home. The salmon-coloured road, serpentine shoreline, and verdant scenery, featuring a blend of white pine, ash, birch, and other trees native to Nova Scotia seem to directly allude to the Annapolis Valley, with its distinctive iron-rich red alluvial soil. The Annapolis Royal-Granville Ferry communities were important export-import centres in the early 1800s, and improved methods of transport and communication put them in direct contact with the leading Atlantic ports of Halifax and Saint John. By 1816 the two main roads linking Pictou and Annapolis to Halifax had been completed and from the 1820s the Western Stage Company provided a stagecoach service for passengers and mail, covering the stretch between Annapolis Royal and Halifax in eight hours.[55] All types of vessels from various Canadian and American east coast ports, notably Boston, regularly anchored in the harbour of Annapolis Royal. Steamboats, as depicted in the painting, provided a ferry service across the Bay of Fundy to Saint John from 1826, and

34.
"Annapolis Royal," by J.F.W. Desbarres et al, etching with aquatint dated c. 1775, published in *The Atlantic Neptune*, London, around 1777–81. Desbarres's etching shows the early docking facilities at Annapolis Royal, indicated by the full-rigged ship along the far shore, seen just below the overhang of the trees in the left foreground. These docks appear in similar proximity to the flag-topped citadel in the Croscup artist's painting of an Atlantic harbour scene. Collection: National Archives of Canada (C 2705).

36.

35.

"Old Fort, near Annapolis Royal (Nova Scotia)," engraved by J. Cousen after a drawing by William H. Bartlett, published by N.P. Willis in *Canadian Scenery Illustrated*, London, 1842. This print, based on a drawing made during Bartlett's 1838 tour of the Canadas, depicts the view across the Annapolis Basin toward Digby Gut, more or less as it appears from the south shore citadel, site of the old fort of Annapolis Royal. The distant shoreline is similar to that painted by the Croscup artist. Collection: National Gallery of Canada.

36.

The Town and Harbour of Halifax Looking Up to the King's Yard and Basin, drawn by Richart Short in 1759, engraved by James Mason, published by John Boydell, London, 25 April 1777. The Croscup artist had obvious difficulties in establishing spatial and proportional relationships when not working from a complete secondary source. It is possible, therefore, that his Atlantic harbour mural is a telescoped and simplified rendering of the port of Halifax from the southeast channel looking inland toward Bedford Basin, as in Short's drawing here (compare *fig. 36*). The geographical relationship of the northern tip of McNab's Island (foreground) to the Halifax harbourfront and the distant citadel is closer than the Bartlett drawing *(fig. 34)* to the arrangement of land masses and harbourfront in the Croscup panel. Collection: Royal Ontario Museum, Toronto (960x66.18).

37.

between Granville Ferry and Annapolis Royal from 1830.[56] The Croscup artist's rendering is thus not out of keeping with the realities of this region in the 1840s.

For all these points of similarity, however, it cannot be said for certain that the north mural was intended to portray Annapolis Royal and environs. The port buildings, including the commercial and religious structures, are rendered with such attention to detail that they do suggest actual buildings, yet extant maps and pictures of the region cannot provide enough information about the port architecture of Annapolis Royal at this time to allow for a clear identification of the site as such. The clapboard and shingle construction of the waterfront warehouses, the Neo-Gothic styling of the church steeples, and the distinctive crib-wharves are at least sufficient to establish the locale as that of a northeastern Atlantic coastal town.

37.
Halifax Harbour Seen from McNab's Island, 1840–60, by Westcott Witchurch Lyttleton. Watercolour and gouache over pencil, 31.9 × 76.8 cm. Collection: Royal Ontario Museum, Toronto (960x276.121).

One major problem of identification concerns the position of the stretch of shoreline in the right foreground in relation to the town wharves in the painting, which is not accurate if the scene is supposed to represent the north shore of the Annapolis Basin and Annapolis Royal to the south. It more closely resembles, in this sense, the port of Halifax viewed from the southeastern perspective of McNab's Island, rendered, for example, in a 1777 engraving by James Mason, after a drawing by Richard Short from 1759 *(fig. 36)*, and in a watercolour by Westcott Witchurch Lyttleton (1818–1886) produced between 1840 and 1860 *(fig. 37)*. Halifax also had a steam ferry service to Dartmouth. Not insignificantly, the direction in which the paddlewheeler steams toward the port in the Croscup panel is like that of the Halifax-Dartmouth ferry seen from McNab's Island. The hilltop signal tower in the painting is also more convincing as a representation of Signal Hill, Halifax, than of the old fort on the rocky promontory overlooking Annapolis Royal. Furthermore, the royal naval dockyards were located just a short distance north of the Halifax ferry slip. Could the ship being launched in the Croscup mural represent a locally built British naval vessel? Or is it an Atlantic commercial packet? Both classes of ship could bear the red ensign at this time, and fake gunports were still commonly painted on the sides of larger commercial vessels in the 1830s and 1840s – vestiges of earlier days when they served to warn off marauding privateers.

Signal flags on the ships and on the hilltop, which would normally provide information about the identity of the vessels and the port itself, have been rendered purely decorative by the Croscup artist, so there are no clues to confirm the identity of the port. The design of the ships' flags, like the forms of the vessels they adorn, was apparently inspired by engravings from *The Illustrated London News* which again served as prototypes. The ship being launched, the paddlewheeler in the foreground, the tugboat towing out the ship, and the first schooner behind the ship were clearly all derived from the wood engraving illustrating the launching of *The Wellesley* at Blackwall, outside London, England, published in *The Illustrated London News* of 13 April 1844 *(fig. 38)*. A print entitled "Towing Out" in the same issue, depicting the ship *St. Vincent* embarking from Deptford to Plymouth, England, to receive emigrants bound for Sydney, Australia, was

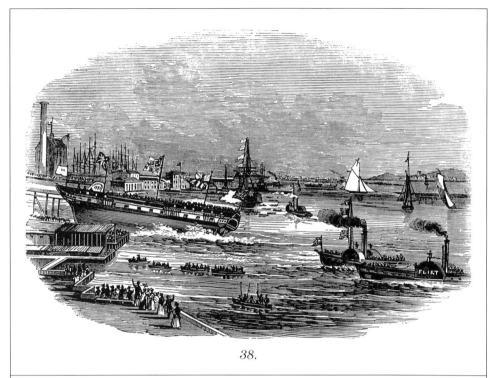

38.

38.
"Launch of 'The Wellesley,' at Blackwall," engraving in *The Illustrated London News*, 13 April 1844. Collection: National Library of Canada.

39.

39.
"Towing Out," engraving in *The Illustrated London News*, 13 April 1844. Collection: National Library of Canada.

40.
"Mr. Day's 'The Ugly Buck,' and
Lord George Bentinck's 'The Devil
to Pay' – Race for 2000 Guineas,
at Newmarket," engraving in
The Illustrated London News,
13 May 1844. Collection: National
Library of Canada.

40.

the prototype for the ship under tow and for the positioning of
the tugboat *(fig. 39)*.[57]

In a quite sophisticated operation, the artist managed to fit
all these vessels into the narrow channel between the harbourfront and the shore in the near right foreground. To properly
integrate them into their new pictorial context, the direction in
which the flags fly from the masts and taffrail of the ship under
tow was reversed from the printed image to conform with those
on the other boats. By contrast, the red flag atop the signal mast
on the hill is shown waving in the opposite direction, most
likely to balance its slightly off-centre position between the two
flanking steeples.

Complementing the central shipping scene highlighting
Maritime commercial activities, the foreground accents local
social pursuits – "match horse racing" (with paired horses) and
a private fishing party. The group of boys fishing, the dense
screen of trees to the right, and the slope of land merging into
the road at the bottom appear to be wholly the product of artistic
invention. The racehorses and riders, on the other hand, were
modelled after an illustration in *The Illustrated London News*
(13 May 1844) of a match race at the famous Newmarket race-
course in England *(fig. 40)*.[58] Consequently, these latter figures
are painted with a better sense of proportion and substance than

the rather tentative forms of the fisherboys or the ghostly spectators crowding the wharves and ship decks. Transplanted to North America by British immigrants, horse racing was very popular in various Atlantic communities from the late eighteenth century. Match racing and, in particular, flat racing (run on a level course) were well organized in Nova Scotia and devotees enjoyed quality matches in the years between 1825 – when the Halifax Turf Club was established – and 1850.[59]

As in previously cited instances in which painted images were copied from prints, the forms in the north wall panel were generally simplified, with some details omitted or added as the artist pleased. Two notable alterations, for example, involve the addition of the name *JUNO LONDON* to the stern of the ship under tow, and the replacement of the name *FLIRT* (as seen in the print) for *FLIGHT* on the paddlewheel cover of the steamboat in the foreground. Given this original application of names, one might think that the vessels represented were known to the artist or the Croscups, and maybe they were. However, a steam-powered boat named *FLIGHT* was never registered as operating in Canadian waters and, although a brigantine named *JUNO* was built in Granville, Nova Scotia, in 1839, launched in August of that year and subsequently sold in Belfast, Ireland, in 1841, William Croscup's name does not appear on the registration document either as the builder or the owner.[60] The continuing quandary about the specific location of the Croscup maritime scene leads to the more likely conclusion that it is not a documentary representation at all but rather an imaginative recreation of life in a typical Nova Scotia coastal community of the 1840s.

SOUTH WALL: RURAL INTERLUDE

The paintings on the north wall relate thematically to the three murals separated by the two windows on the south, which similarly represent familiar views of the people and land of Nova Scotia (*pl. 4*). The panel to the left shows a Micmac family encamped in a forest. This composition appears to be entirely original, probably recreated from memory.

41.
"The General's Bridge, near Annapolis (Nova Scotia)," steel engraving, drawn by William H. Bartlett in 1838 and engraved by J.C. Bentley. First published by N.P. Willis in *Canadian Scenery Illustrated*, London, 1842. Collection: National Gallery of Canada.

41.

As evidenced in the 1842 engraving, "The General's Bridge, near Annapolis (Nova Scotia)" after a drawing by W.H. Bartlett *(fig. 41)*, one could still encounter seasonal Micmac camps in the forests of the Annapolis Valley during the 1840s. Gradually pushed off their traditional hunting and fishing grounds by the growing immigrant population and decimated by its diseases, the Micmacs roamed Nova Scotia, in numbers much reduced by the mid-nineteenth century. The Croscups' Micmac neighbours would, for the most part, have been somewhat peripheral figures colouring the background of life in prospering Annapolis Valley communities. Describing the scene illustrated in Bartlett's drawing, N.P. Willis reflects romantically on the "picturesque character" of the encampment of Micmac people – a prevailing artistic view in these years.[61] The Croscup artist's rendering of his subjects is, however, neither romantic nor clinical. Within the limits of his skills, his depiction is a realistic one, made familiar to occupants of the house by its emphasis on family life, the virtues of which were eulogized by contemporary Victorians.

The special attention paid by the artist to the physical appearance of the figures, their costumes, and the traditionally designed handcrafted possessions, notably the birchbark canoe, bears witness to his keen ethnographic interest in his subject. Although these are not portraits, the characteristic physical traits of the Micmac people – unique facial structure, dark skin, straight black hair – have been quite convincingly captured, despite the artist's obvious difficulties in rendering forms, particularly human anatomy, with a real sense of weight, volume, and proportion. Their possessions, in turn, are pictured in such detail that each item and the materials of which it is made may be quickly identified by modern ethnographers.[62] A similar documentary approach to the subject is to be found in a nearly contemporary oil painting, *Micmac Indians (fig. 42)*.

In another interpretation of life in Nova Scotia's remaining wilderness, the central mural features a hunter and his dog on a path leading into a stand of trees similar in type and shape to those in the two flanking panels. Although the scene was probably intended to represent one of the common outdoor activities of Nova Scotians, the actual figure of the hunter was modelled after that of Prince Albert in an engraving entitled "Buck Shooting in the Highlands" of 3 September 1842 in *The Illustrated London News (fig. 43)*[63] – itself probably inspired by the famous stag hunting paintings of Edwin Landseer.[64]

The artist's interest in the engraving of the prince evidently extended only to his appearance here as a hunter, for no attempt to identify the painted figure as the famous royal personage has been made. The general form and relaxed pose of the prince in the engraving have been reproduced, along with many of the details of his accoutrements, including the long-barrelled rifle, although the face of the hunter in the mural is transformed into that of a clean-shaven younger man with a more elongated head and a smooth, rosy complexion. The prince's Glengarry cap has also been changed into a high-crowned hat with a nondescript plaid pattern. At the figure's feet a hunting dog, primarily of the artist's own creation, alertly turns his head as if catching sight of passing prey. The lush landscape, featuring a variety of coniferous and deciduous trees, is very much like that of Nova Scotia. Broadly rendered, each tree is nonetheless quite distinctive in form, generally corresponding in type and placement to those

42.
Micmac Indians, oil on panel, painted in the mid-nineteenth century by an unknown Canadian artist. As in the Croscup panel, the pictorial emphasis is placed on the unique lifestyle, dress, and possessions of the Micmac, with close attention to design and decorative effects. Note the painter's strikingly similar approach to that of the Croscup artist in the placement of the canoes in the foreground and the odd cropping of one of the craft. The woman with her child in the centre canoe, like the Micmac mother in the Croscup panel, faces the viewer, making a personal contact that draws one into the scene. Collection: National Gallery of Canada.

43.
"Buck Shooting in the Highlands," engraving in *The Illustrated London News*, 3 September 1842. Collection: National Archives of Canada.

42.

43.

found in the other two south murals. The visual link in all three is the similar composition, with three basic receding planes and shared horizon lines, as well as a common earth-toned colour scheme.

The third panel, to the right, presents a peaceful landscape with a small waterfall in the foreground. Framing the scene on the left and filling the upper half of the panel is a large branching tree. The arching leafless lower branches and the rocky shore on the right help to guide the eye toward the green rolling terrain in the distance. Near the shore stands a simple gabled house, similar in design to the one depicted in the decorative landscape directly opposite on the north wall *(pl. 2)*. Here, as in the other south wall panels, the definition of space is ambiguous. The artist has sought to create the illusion of receding space through the judicious placement, diminution, and successively paler treatment of objects moving hazily into the distance. Yet the high, narrow format of each panel and the planar composition still tend to invite a vertical reading of each picture in contrast with the linear perspective of the city and harbour subjects on the west and north walls.

A UNIQUE VISION

The principal themes traced in the Croscup murals reflect the main concerns of early Victorian society. Home and family, central Victorian institutions, are the focus of attention in the three murals of Queen Victoria and her family, a mother and child, and a Micmac family. In the Victorian "cult of home," the home was seen as a protective, comforting haven for its members against the incursions of the harsh, outside world. It was also the seat of the family which, in the ideal scenario, provided essential moral support and guidance and a sense of security and continuity in an era of sweeping social change. The positive experiences of family life and the emotional bonds between parents, children, and siblings were regarded, within the context of this Victorian ethic, as universal, transcending financial, social, national, and racial barriers – a notion conveyed through the three views of family life in the Croscup room as seen, respectively, in high social circles, a provincial bourgeois household, and Native North American society.[65]

The merits and rewards of work for the individual good and for society at large was another firmly ingrained Victorian belief, both in Britain and North America. The promotion of a dominant work ethic, emphasizing hard and honest labour, self-help, discipline, perseverance, and economy, was assisted by the literary and visual arts through graphic descriptions of the personal and social progress achieved through such enterprise. In the Croscup room, contemporary attitudes to work and its fruitful consequences find expression in scenes of modern urban development, as in the views of London and Saint Petersburg and the Atlantic port. By contrast, the pictures of a Scottish piper apparently entertaining three fashionable women, the sportsman and his dog, and the vignettes of horse racing and fishing represent common recreational activities.

A visual dialogue about nature and humanity may also be followed through the various scenes, from studies highlighting individuals in harmony with their environment (the Micmac family), to rural industry (the harbour scene), to complete dominance over nature (the cityscapes). With the exception of the overmantel piece, the paintings all represent outdoor locales or activities taking place out of doors. Throughout, nature is portrayed in a benevolent mood, as on a sunny, midsummer day. No attempt has been made to capture the provincial landscape in any other season. Consequently the walls are filled with rich green flora in full leaf, contributing to the lush, warm atmosphere of the small, intimate parlour. Skies are clear and the winds calm, when they are not propelling sailing vessels or snapping flags. Within this idyllic environment, the frequent wet and wintry days on the Annapolis Basin shores could easily be forgotten by the Croscups and their visitors.

In their use of interior spaces and in their taste in design and decoration, the Croscup family, like most English-speaking Canadians and their American neighbours, were obviously influenced by British social habits and design concepts. Certain common aesthetic concerns discerned in the parlour decor may be traced in other European and North American domestic interiors decorated in the 1840s and 1850s. Viewed in relation to defined "high culture" styles of this period, the Croscup decor may be considered stylistically transitional. Typical of many decorated interiors produced during the early years of Queen Victoria's reign, it displays an ongoing allegiance to Regency aesthetic ideals while also expressing newer Victorian tastes. The sense of solidity, rational organization, and formal restraint in the decorative scheme reflects an adherence to the classical principles of Regency design. At the same time, one may observe a resurgent love for richly coloured, textured, and formally varied ornamentation that is characteristically Victorian. The Croscup artist also adopts the eclectic approach whereby interesting pictorial subjects and decorative ideas from different sources are reworked within a new context. While common among folk painters, this aesthetic informed the work of high-fashion Victorian interior decorators.

There is a Regency-like simplicity and lightness to the Croscup decor, achieved through a careful regulation of the number, type, and organization of the decorative elements, that is comparable in effect to many early nineteenth-century British and North American domestic interiors (fig. 44). These qualities may be better understood when the Croscup parlour, albeit missing its original furnishings, is seen in light of the richly coloured, opulently textured Victorian interiors produced after 1860 (fig. 45).

Although it displays certain formal affinities with contemporary decorated interiors, the Croscup decor cannot be conveniently classified. On the one hand, the murals reveal a degree of artistic knowledge and practical skill on the part of the painter-decorator that indicates they are the work of an artist with a significant amount of professional training. In addition, in the choice and nature of the subjects, the attitude taken toward pictorial space – rendered in most areas in three dimensions according to the laws of perspective – and the complex yet homogeneous organization of the varied pictorial components, the murals approach the academic product. At the same time, they display a formal naïvety and preoccupation with design in and for itself which links the room more with traditional decorative folk art.

The manner in which the Croscup artist represents his subjects tends also to breach simple stylistic classifications, lying somewhere between the polar limits of two broad categories of

44.
A view of the parlour in the French-Robertson House, originally located at Maple Grove, Mille Roches, Upper Canada, now preserved at Upper Canada Village. The house was built by Jeremiah French around 1784 as a simple timber frame building which survives today as the dining room. The first structure was later enlarged to accommodate the families of George Robertson, who bought it in 1812, and his son, George Jr. The elegant parlour interior, restored to the year 1820, features a floral wallpaper with trompe-l'œil drapery borders dating from about 1819 and closely resembling a paper produced by the English firm of Cowtan and Sons. Collection: Upper Canada Village, Morrisburg, Ont.

45.
Parlour of the Trafalgar House, Montreal, in a William Notman photo of 1887. Collection: Notman Photographic Archives, McCord Museum, Montreal.

44.

45.

design, codified by J.C. Loudon as: "...those which are intended to be correct imitations of natural or artificial objects, such as of particular species of plants or animals; and those which are fanciful compositions of artificial forms and lines, or of plants and animals imagined in imitation of nature's general manner, but not copied from any of her specific objects...."[66]

The unusual mix of the imaginary and realistic, decorative and narrative, sophisticated and naïve in the murals is original to the artist. In its design, iconography, and style, the Croscup decor is unique among extant examples of early interior decorative painting in North America. If the name of the Croscup artist remains unknown, his hand is easily distinguished among other provincial painter-decorators active in the mid-nineteenth century.

The specialness of these paintings was evident to the members of the Croscup family who took such good care of the room over the years. Unlike most historic decorated interiors, the parlour walls were never painted or papered over as fashions in interior design changed. Nor were they ever retouched. During her lifetime, Hannah Croscup is said to have strictly supervised visitors to her parlour, banishing unaccompanied children to viewing positions no closer than outside the doorways.[67]

The discovery in January 1981 of scenic murals of comparable design in a house built around 1860 by a relative of the Croscups', John Schaffner (1796–1874), at South Williamston, Nova Scotia, suggests that the Croscups' parlour may have influenced the work of another interior decorator active in northwestern Nova Scotia. John Schaffner lived in this double house with his son, William Judson, and family. The link to the Croscups comes through William Schaffner's wife, Mary Hester Croscup, the daughter of William and Hannah. It has been suggested that the decoration of the South Williamston house, probably about 1865, may have been done to please the younger Mrs Schaffner, who had grown up in the Croscup home at Karsdale. The key points of resemblance between the two painted interiors help support this theory.[68]

Like the Croscup room, the decorative ensemble in the Schaffner house features floor-length scenic oil murals, nine in all, which cover the plastered walls in a series of individual panels set within an architectural framework of simulated grained

46.
Mural, oil on plaster, dated
c. 1865, on the on east parlour
wall of the Schaffner House,
South Williamston, N.S.
To the right, a schooner under
construction.

46.

wood trim. The subjects of these murals are also similar in type, including marine scenes – notably a ship under construction in drydock – architectural studies, and pastoral landscapes *(figs. 46 – 48)*. Most telling is the Schaffner artist's use of *The Illustrated London News* engravings from 1842 as prototypes for two, possibly three, of the murals.[69]

Within a month of the discovery of the Schaffner murals, another set was uncovered in a house at Bear River, a community just southwest of Karsdale where more Croscup and Schaffner family members lived in the mid-1800s. In February 1981 an opportunity arose to remove the wallpaper down to the plaster in a corner of one of the walls in the Bear River house that contained an alcove.[70] The mural uncovered on the alcove wall conformed with a 1922 description of this decor *(fig. 49)* reportedly painted "…by a famous English artist who visited Halifax for a considerable period and went to Bear River on fishing trips."[71] Six individual murals, mistakenly attributed at this time to Nova

47.

47.
Mural, oil on plaster, dated
c. 1865, on the west parlour wall
of the Schaffner House, South
Williamston, N.S. To the left, a
landscape with a stone castle;
to the right, a bridge over
a river.

48.

49.

48.
Mural, oil on plaster, dated
c. 1865, on the east parlour wall
of the Schaffner House, South
Williamston, N.S.

49.
Mural, oil on plaster, dated
c. 1850, in the alcove of a house
at Bear River, N.S. The design
is thought to be after the wood

engraving "View of Clermont"
in *The Illustrated London News*,
31 December 1842.

Scotia artist John Slayter, Jr (1746–1824), were then visible. According to Elmer Morgan, Secretary of the Bear River branch of The Great War Veterans' Association, then occupying the house: "… The paintings have been passed on as oil paintings. They are six separate paintings. The room is about 16 feet square. Over the mantle [sic] – 4 × 5 feet – is *Halifax with Harbour & Dartmouth*…. Also one in an alcove which in my opinion represents our building & front at the time when seen by the artist. 3 × 3 feet…. The walls of the room are painted to represent a Castle with Bridge, boat & stream, landscape views & deer stalking…."[72]

The alcove painting (the only panel yet exposed) does indeed depict a tree-filled rural landscape with a large two-storey Georgian-style house. Rather than depicting the Bear River building, however, it is thought to represent "Claremont," the English country residence of the Prince Regent's daughter, Princess Charlotte, based on yet another print from *The Illustrated London News* of 31 December 1842.[73]

Although the practice of working from published prints, the painting technique, basic design concerns, and general pictorial interests are similar, the Schaffner and Bear River artists were clearly more amateur-class decorators than the Croscup artist. Their work is weaker by virtue of the poorer draftsmanship and inferior comprehension of the physical realities of many of their subjects. Their murals lack the vibrancy, harmony, and joyous tone of the Karsdale decor, which only serves to highlight the extraordinary achievement of the Croscup artist.

APPENDIX

Restoration and Conservation of the Painted Parlour

* The conservation team included: (Phase 1) Edward Kulka, Sandra Lawrence, Diane McKay, Joe Marceau, Barbara Ramsay, Mervyn Ruggles, A. Erwin Stehr; (Phase 2) Margaret Bignell, Laurie Hamilton, Barbara Ramsay; (Phase 3) Wendy Baker, Virginia Caswell, Anne Maheux, Barbara Ramsay, Cathy Stewart, Adele Trussler. (Phase 4, reinstallation) Maurice Bastien, Calvin Franklin, J. MacGregor Grant, Laurier Marion, Claude Saumure, Hector Richer, and François Hamel. A detailed report on the examination and treatment of the Croscup room may be found in Ian Hodkinson, "Conservation and Transfer of an Early 19th Century Painted Room," *The Association for Preservation Technology Bulletin*, XIV:1 (1982), pp. 17–35.

As it is always preferable, when possible, to preserve a work of art in its original context, the controversial decision to remove the murals from the Croscup-Hall House in Karsdale, Nova Scotia, was reached only after much thought and consultation. The rapidly deteriorating condition of the paintings and the owner's wishes were carefully considered. Discussions were also carried out with the Nova Scotia government, whose limited resources at the time regrettably prevented it from responding positively to local appeals for assistance to keep the Croscup room in the province.

The National Gallery's conservation team determined that transfer, rather than conservation *in situ*, was the most practical course of action. This decision, of course, meant divorcing the paintings from the larger context of the original house. But by preserving not only the walls but also the floor, fireplace, windows, doors, and architectural trim, and reassembling the entire room (except for the original ceiling and doors) in the National Gallery, the murals can still be understood and appreciated within the specific architectural setting for which they were conceived and to which they intimately relate.

Work on the Croscup room was carried out over a four-year period by a team of graduate students in the Master of Art Conservation program at Queen's University. The team was supervised by Ian Hodkinson, Professor of Fine Art Conservation at Queen's, in collaboration with staff from the National Gallery's Restoration and Conservation Laboratory and the Technical Services Workshop. Their prodigious task was carried out in four main stages: (1) examination, consolidation, and removal of the paintings and other room elements; (2) attachment of new supports to the plaster panels; (3) removal of temporary facings and old varnish layers and restoration of the painted surface; (4) reassembly of the room in the National Gallery. The conservation team arrived in Karsdale in the spring of 1976 to begin the first phase.*

50.

50.
Interior of the Croscups'
painted parlour shortly before
dismantling. The view is of the
west wall, with Victorian
furnishings.

A thorough examination and report on the condition of the murals preceded any action by team members. Plan and elevation drawings, extensive photographic records, diagrams, and written accounts documented every portion of the room in detail. It was established at this stage that, except for periodic varnishing, the paintings had been left almost untouched, and no previous restoration had been attempted. However, after more than 125 years the murals were in an advanced state of deterioration brought about by the gradual settling of the building, oscillating Relative Humidity levels, atmospheric pollution, and the deleterious effects of water and light. There had also been heat damage, caused by a new forced hot-air system installed three years earlier *(fig. 50).* *

To arrest the active lifting and flaking of paint before removing the plaster walls it was necessary to consolidate the paint layers. This was done with a mixture of organic solvents and a stable, synthetic resin adhesive (Paraloid B-72) that softened the flaking paint and bonded it to the plaster support. In the same operation a layer of tissue, the first of three temporary protective facings, was applied to the fragile painted surface with Paraloid B-72. The same adhesive was used to attach a second facing layer of polyester gauze. A top facing of strong, medium-weight linen canvas was bonded to the tissue and gauze with Italian *colletta* or hide glue mixture. As a final measure, a urethane foam-lined plywood cover was applied to ensure maximum protection of the paintings during transfer.

The removal of the doors, windows, architraves, baseboards, mantelpiece, and floorboards preceded removal of the painted plaster walls. Once the murals were triple-faced, they were divided into twelve numbered panels, following natural crack lines as much as possible. Cuts were made in the plaster only where necessary and as inconspicuously as possible – for example, above doorways and along ceiling/wall joins. Depending on the size of the panels and accessibility to the back of the wall, the murals were detached in one of three ways: either by removing the plaster only; the plaster and lath together; or the plaster, lath, and wall studs. The faced murals were then lowered to the floor and the lath, wall studs, and plaster keying, as applicable, were cut away from the back of the plaster in preparation for crating and transport *(fig. 51).* To provide sufficient space for the plywood crates to be brought out to the truck, the west wall of the house had to be opened.** (The house has since been reconstructed to the owner's specifications.)

The next stage of the project took place in the Conservation Laboratory at Queen's University. First, to strengthen the fragile plaster murals, now divested of wood lath, and to permit them to be moved

* Hodkinson, p. 17.
** Ibid, pp. 22–23.

51.

East wall of the Croscup room after the murals had received the initial facing of tissue and the mantelpiece, baseboards, and other architectural trim had been removed. The horizontal wood lath support is visible around the plaster panels.

and reassembled with ease, a new support was attached to the sections. This was made of a lightweight aluminum honeycomb, with fibreglass-reinforced polyester resin backing and a basswood strip frame. Only after this step was completed could the temporary protective facings be removed and surface cleaning begin in the National Gallery's Restoration and Conservation Laboratory (fig. 52). Finally, came the exciting phase of varnish removal, as with the progressive elimination of yellowed coats of old varnish the original paint surface was revealed. Transformed by cleaning, the palette of the Croscup artist proved to be much more vibrant and colourful than one could have imagined under the previously discoloured surface.

To minimize the disruptive visual effect created by areas of missing paint, infilling of losses and inpainting in a reversible medium were subsequently carried out, though this was restricted to places in which the artist's intention was obvious or in areas of paint loss resulting from the transfer of the murals. All natural cracks and defects in the paint caused by drying of the plaster or the paint layers or by the settling of the building were not restored. Large paint losses in areas in which the

52.
National Gallery conservator
Barbara Ramsay-Jolicœur removes
surface dirt and old varnish from
the north wall ship launching
panel in the Gallery's Restoration
and Conservation Laboratory,
1979.

52.

artist's intent was no longer obvious were either left untouched or simply filled and tinted to blend in with the surrounding colour. The *trompe l'œil* curtain that framed the paintings was found to have been coloured with a fugitive organic red pigment and was so faded that it was decided not to retouch it. After restoration the murals were then protected with a clear coating of Paraloid B-72 resin varnish.*

The unit approach adopted during the dismantling of the room, along with the new support system developed for the murals, greatly facilitated reassembly of all architectural elements by the National Gallery preparators. In December 1980 the painted room was opened for public viewing in the Early Canadian galleries on the third floor of the Gallery's former Elgin Street home. It remained on exhibit there until March 1987, when preparations began for the move to the new Gallery building on Sussex Drive. The present permanent installation has been enhanced by the addition of the original external door mouldings and by a reorientation of the walls so that one is now able to see through the two south-facing windows which formerly afforded a panoramic view of the Annapolis Basin.

* Hodkinson, op cit, p. 34.

Chapter 1

1. To become a Freeman of the City of New York on 20 June 1769, Ludwick swore allegiance to the British Crown and accepted the Anglican faith. Within a year of the signing of the Treaty of Paris in 1783, resolving the American Revolution in favour of the New England colonies, the Croscup family, including the first four of eight children, emigrated north of the new British-American border to the Annapolis Valley. National Gallery of Canada, Curatorial File, "Croscup Room (18688)," Cora Greenaway, unpublished manuscript, 1988, pp. 2, 4–6.

2. Ibid, pp. 6–10.

3. National Gallery of Canada, Curatorial File, op cit, Greenaway, unpublished manuscript, 1979, chap., "Croscup Family History," pp. 6, 11.

4. Public Archives of Nova Scotia (hereafter PANS), MG4, no. 34, Granville Parish, Records of Marriage, 1814–1882, p. 58. Early spellings of the Schaffner name were: "Schafner," or "Shafner."

5. Ibid; National Gallery of Canada, Curatorial File, op cit, Greenaway, unpublished manuscript, 1988, p. 11.

6. PANS, MG4, no. 34, Records of Granville Township 1779–1876, p. 49.

7. Inscription on Hannah Croscup's tombstone, Christ Church Cemetery, Karsdale, N.S.

8. Inscription on William Croscup's tombstone, Christ Church Cemetery, Karsdale, N.S.

9. Bridgetown, Registry of Deeds, Book 37, p. 250; Cora Greenaway, "Decorated Walls and Ceilings in Nova Scotia," *Material History Bulletin*, no. 15 (Summer 1982), pp. 83, 88 n. 3; PANS, RG47, Quit Claim Deed, 13 June 1960, vol. 222, p. 575; National Gallery of Canada, Curatorial File, op cit, Greenaway, unpublished manuscript, 1979, chap., "The Croscup Family," p. 7.

10. See Peter Ennals and Deryck Holdsworth, "Vernacular Architecture and the Cultural Landscape of the Maritime Provinces – A Reconnaissance," *Atlantic Canada before Confederation, The Acadiensis Reader*, vol. 1, edited by P.A. Buckner and David Frank (Fredericton: Acadiensis Press, 1985), pp. 341–43.

11. "The Hall-Croscup House," in Heritage Trust of Nova Scotia, *Seasoned Timbers: A Sampling of Historic Buildings Unique to Western Nova Scotia* (Halifax: Heritage Trust of Nova Scotia, 1972), p. 110.

12. Ibid.

13. National Gallery of Canada, Curatorial File, letter from Mrs Marion Beard to Cora Greenaway, 26 Mar 1984.

14. See Nina Fletcher Little, *American Decorative Wall Painting, 1700–1850* (New York: E.P. Dutton & Co. Inc., 1972), pp. 20, 93; Robert L. McGrath, *Early Vermont Wall Paintings, 1790–1850* (Hanover, N.H.: The University Press of New England, 1972), p. 80; Jean Lipman, *Rufus Porter, Yankee Pioneer* (New York: Clarkson N. Potter Inc., 1968), p. 93; Edward B. Allen, *Early American Wall Paintings, 1710–1850* (New York: Kennedy Graphics, Inc., Da Capo Press, 1971), pp. 12, 63, 78; Jean Lipman and Alice Winchester, *The Flowering of American Folk Art, 1776–1876* (New York: The Viking Press, 1974), p. 190.

15. Little, op cit, p. 17.

16. Nina Fletcher Little attributes the overmantel painting to Connecticut painter Jared Jessup (active in the first quarter of the 19th century). See Little, op cit, p. 58, fig. 56.

17. The Adam style swept England in the 1760s and 1770s, quickly spreading across the Atlantic toward the end of the century. See Damie Stillman, *The Decorative Work of Robert Adam* (London: Alec Tiranti, 1966); James Lees-Milne, *The Age of Adam* (London: B.T. Batsford, 1947); John Swarbrick, *Robert Adam and His Brothers* (London: B.T. Batsford, 1915).

18. Felicity L. Leung, *Wall Paper in Canada, 1600s–1930s*, Microfiche Report Series No. 208 (Ottawa: Parks Canada, 1983), passim.

19. See E.A. Entwisle, *French Scenic Wallpapers, 1800–1860* (Leigh-on-Sea, England: F. Lewis Publishers Limited, 1972).

20. Jean Gordon Forbes, "History and Romance of Wall-paper," *The Canadian Magazine*, LXIII:8 (Dec 1924), pp. 465–70; Leung,

op cit, pp. 92–93; Arthur W. Wallace, *An Album of Drawings of Early Buildings in Nova Scotia* (Halifax: Heritage Trust of Nova Scotia and Nova Scotia Museum, 1976), pl. 52; Entwisle, op cit, p. 37, figs. 28, 29.

21. Walter Abell, "An Introduction to Canadian Architecture," *Canadian Geographical Journal*, XXXIV:6 (June 1947), p. 262; Leung, op cit, p. 94.

22. "John Bowles," *The Acadian Recorder*, 5 Aug 1815, p. 3.

23. Smithers & Studley, *Monthly Advertiser (Halifax Monthly Magazine* supplement) II:17 (1 Oct 1831).

24. Jeanne Minhinnick, *At Home in Upper Canada* (Toronto/Vancouver: Clarke, Irwin & Co. Ltd., 1970), pp. 124–27.

25. Leung, op cit, p. 88.

26. Rufus Porter, "The Art of Painting – Landscape Painting on Walls of Rooms," *Scientific American*, no. 21 (5 Feb 1846), p. 2.

27. Minhinnick, op cit, illus. p. 127; Michael Bird, "Folk Art on Walls," *The Upper Canadian*, IV:6 (Jul/Aug 1984), pp. 24–25.

28. Information about this stencilled room has been kindly supplied by Cora Greenaway, who first discovered it in 1987. For historical background on the house, see Charlotte Isabella Perkins, *The Romance of Old Annapolis Royal, Nova Scotia* (5th reprint of 1925 edition, Historical Association of Annapolis Royal, 1985), pp. 29–30.

29. See Lipman, op cit.

30. Rufus Porter, "The Art of Painting – Imitation Painting," *Scientific American*, no. 17 (8 Jan 1846), p. 2.

31. J.C. Loudon, *An Encyclopædia of Cottage, Farm and Villa Architecture and Furniture* (London: Longman, Rees, Orme, Brown, Green & Longman, 1833), p. 227.

32. Porter, op cit, no. 17, p. 2.

33. See Michael Bird and Terry Kobayashi, "The Discovery of Thomas MacDonald, Canada's Elusive Portrait Painter," *The Clarion*, XIII:1 (Winter 1988), pp. 37–43.

34. Cora Greenaway, *Interior Decorative Painting in Nova Scotia* (Halifax: Art Gallery of Nova Scotia, 1986), cat. no. 6, p. 36 illus.

35. See note 14.

Chapter 2

36. Ian Hodkinson, "Conservation and Transfer of an Early 19th Century Painted Room," *The Association for Preservation Technology Bulletin*, XIV:1 (1982), p. 20.

37. Gilbert L. Gignac and Jeanne L. L'Espérance, "Thoughts of Peace and Joy: A Study of the Iconography of the Croscup Room," *The Journal of Canadian Art History*, VI:2 (1982), pp. 173–75.

38. Ibid, pp. 175–76.

39. See: C. Kurt Dewhurst, Betty MacDowell, and Marsha MacDowell, *Artists in Aprons: Folk Art by American Women* (New York: E.P. Dutton in association with the Museum of American Folk Art, 1979).

40. Hannah Croscup lived until 1913 so that several of her great-grandchildren, still living in the 1970s, had the opportunity to meet her. It is reasonable to expect that if Hannah had taken any part in decorating her parlour, which everyone knew to be her great pride, this would have been communicated to younger family members. The Croscups' descendants, headed by great-granddaughter Mrs Marion Beard, strongly dispute the notion that Hannah was the artist, citing the fact that she was the only female adult living in the Karsdale family home at the time the murals were most likely painted. By 1845, William and Hannah's sisters were either married with their own households or unmarried and living in their parents' homes. National Gallery of Canada, Curatorial File, op cit, Greenaway, unpublished manuscript, 1979, Croscup Genealogy, pp. 2–5, Schaffner Genealogy, p. 2; letter from Mrs Marion Beard to Cora Greenaway, 26 Mar 1984.

41. Gignac and L'Espérance, op cit, p. 144.

42. Ibid, p. 147.

43. This was first noted by Gilbert Gignac and Jeanne L'Espérance, op cit, p. 148.

44. Mrs Hale, "Queen Victoria's Treasures," *Godey's Lady's Magazine* (Feb 1844), p. 59.

45. Gignac and L'Espérance, op cit, p. 151.

46. "Visit of the King of the French to England," *The Nova Scotian*, 19 Aug 1844, p. 275. An article about the life and career of Louis-Philippe had been published on 4 Dec 1843 in *The Nova Scotian*, p. 388.

47. "The Life of Louis-Philippe," *The Times*, London, 8 Oct 1844, p. 5; "The Visit of the King of the French," *The Times*, London, 9 Oct 1844, pp. 4–5; "The King of the French," *The Illustrated London News*, 12 Oct 1844, p. 233; Barbara Scott, "Guest of the Queen: Louis Philippe at Windsor," Part I, *Country Life*, 10 Nov 1983, p. 1316.

48. As told to Cora Greenaway by one of Hannah Croscup's great-grandchildren, W. Reginald Bishop; PANS, MG4, no. 34, Granville Parish, Register of Baptisms, p. 32.

49. A second child, Mary Hester, was born on 22 December 1847. PANS, MG4, Granville Parish, Register of Baptisms, p. 32.

50. *Townsend's Monthly Selection of Parisian Costume*, Oct 1833, no. 106, pl. 521, 523, 524. For more detailed analysis, see Gignac and L'Espérance, op cit, pp. 163–65, 168–69, figs. 28–30.

51. "Martock," for instance, the home of Colonel E.D.S. Butler at Windsor, Nova Scotia, and a hub of regional social activities in the 1840s, featured a similar façade with two ranges of large sash windows and an Ionic portico added in 1846. See Wallace, op cit, plate 64. The Connell House in Woodstock, N.B. (dated 1830–40), of extant pre-1850 buildings in Atlantic Canada, most closely resembles the structure in the Croscup mural, however. Like it, it has a rectangular floor plan with a low gable roof and a distinctive colonnaded porch running the length of the house. The principal difference is that instead of the more decorative Ionic capital, its columns are of the Doric order. Canadian Inventory of Historic Buildings, Historic Sites and Monuments Board of Canada, Environment Canada, File no. 128.

52. Gignac and L'Espérance, op cit, p. 162.

53. Eric W. Sager and Lewis R. Fischer, "Shipping and Shipbuilding in Atlantic Canada 1820–1914," *The Canadian Historical Association Historical Booklet*, no. 42 (Ottawa 1986), pp. 4–7, 12–13; Graeme Wynn, *Timber Colony: A Historical Geography of Early Nineteenth Century New Brunswick* (Toronto: University of Toronto Press, 1981), passim pp. 26–53; Richard Rice, "Shipbuilding in British America 1787–1890, an Introductory Study," unpublished doctoral thesis, University of Liverpool, Dec 1977; David Sutherland, "Halifax Merchants and the Pursuit of Development," *Readings in Canadian History: Pre-Confederation*, edited by R. Douglas Francis and Donald B. Smyth (Toronto: Holt, Rinehart and Winston of Canada, Ltd., 1986) passim pp. 400–13; ibid, T.W. Acheson, "The Great Merchant and Economic Development in St. John 1820–1850," passim pp. 413–35.

54. Sager and Fischer, op cit, p. 4.

55. Joseph Howe, *Western and Eastern Rambles: Travel Sketches of Nova Scotia*, edited by M.G. Parks (Toronto: University of Toronto Press, 1973) pp. 154–55; Michael Cross, "Historical Perspectives, 1780–1930," *Spirit of Nova Scotia: Traditional Decorative Folk Art 1780–1930* (Halifax: Art Gallery of Nova Scotia, 1985), p. 6.

56. W.A. Calnek, *History of the County of Annapolis* (Toronto: William Briggs, 1897; republished Belleville, Ont.: Mika Publishing Company Limited, 1980), p. 283.

57. Gignac and L'Espérance, op cit, pp. 154–55.

58. Op cit, p. 171.

59. Barbara J. Christie, "Flat Racing in Nova Scotia: Testing Ground for Horses of Stamina and Quality)," *The Occasional*, VII:2 (Spring 1982), p. 24.

60. National Archives of Canada, *Ship Register, St. John, N.B.*, 1838–1841, CXXVI:112 (3 Sep 1839).

61. N.P. Wallis, *Canadian Scenery Illustrated* (London: James S. Virtue, 1842), p. 111.

62. See Ruth Holmes Whitehead, *Elitekey: Micmac Material Culture from 1600 A.D. to the Present* (Halifax: Nova Scotia Museum, 1980); Gaby Pelletier, *Micmac and Maliseet Decorative Traditions* (Saint John, N.B.: The New Brunswick Museum, 1977).

63. Gignac and L'Espérance,
op cit, pp. 154–55.

64. The 1827 Landseer oil painting
*Highlanders Returning from
Deer Stalking*, engraved in 1840
by William Finden for the
publication *Royal Gallery of
British Art*, may have been
the prototype for the general
composition and the specific
rendering of the white horse in
the print. The kneeling figures
on the left with the dead buck
could have been inspired by
Landseer's 1824–30 canvas,
*Portraits of His Grace The Duke
of Atoll and George Murray
Attended by His Head Forrester
John Crerar and Keepers* (also
called *Death of a Stag in Glen
Tilt*), engraved in 1833. The
position and pose of Prince
Albert may further be based
on the central figure of George
Murray in this painting, or
on Lord Ossulston as depicted
in Landseer's canvas *Scene in
Chillingham Park: Portrait of Lord
Ossulston* (before 1833–36).
Richard Ormond, *Sir Edwin
Landseer* (exhibition catalogue)
(New York: Rizzoli, 1981), cat.
no. 29 p. 72, cat. no. 30 p. 74,
cat. no. 78 pp. 126–27.

65. Christopher Wood, *Victorian
Panorama: Paintings of Victorian
Life* (London: Faber & Faber
Limited, 1976), pp. 14–15,
19–27, 59–62.

66. Loudon, op cit, p. 279.

67. Information from Mrs Marion
Beard, great-granddaughter,
as told to Cora Greenaway.

68. Cora Greenaway, "Another
Painted Room," *Canadian
Collector*, XVII:3 (May–June
1982), pp. 34–36; Greenaway,
Material History Bulletin,
op cit, pp. 85–87.

69. The west mural depicting
an arched stone bridge was
possibly drawn from an
engraving of Walton Bridge
over the Thames in *The
Illustrated London News*, I:34,
1842 (*see fig. 46*). The east
mural showing a domed
building could be based on a
view of the Capitol Building in
Washington, D.C., in the same
issue (*see fig. 47*). Greenaway,
Canadian Collector, op cit, p. 35.

70. This work was instigated
and supervised by Cora
Greenaway. See Judith Penner,
"Michaelangelo in Overalls,"
Today, 29 May 1982, pp. 6–7.

71. Nova Scotia Museum
Archives, "Vets Discover
Old Paintings," *Echo*, Halifax,
12 Dec 1922.

72. Nova Scotia Museum
Archives, Elmer Morgan,
Secretary and Treasurer,
The Great War Veterans'
Association, Bear River, N.S.,
to Harry Piers, Secretary,
Nova Scotia Historical Society,
Halifax, N.S., 27 Dec 1922.

73. Greenaway, *Canadian Collector*,
op cit, p. 35; Greenaway,
Material History Bulletin,
op cit, p. 87.

Primary Printed Sources

Allen, Edward B. *Early American Wall Paintings, 1710–1850*. New York, Kennedy Graphics Inc., Da Capo Press, 1971.

Armour, Dr Charles A., and Lackey, Thomas. *Sailing Ships of the Maritimes*. Toronto, McGraw-Hill Ryerson Limited, 1975.

Ayres, James. *British Folk Art*. London, Barrie & Jenkins Limited, 1977.

Bird, Michael. "Folk Art on Walls." *The Upper Canadian*, IV:6 (Jul/Aug 1984), pp. 24–25.

Brett, Katherine B. *Modesty to Mod: Dress and Underdress in Canada, 1780–1967*. Toronto, Royal Ontario Museum, 1967.

Burant, Jim. "The Development of the Visual Arts in Halifax, Nova Scotia, from 1815 to 1867 as an Expression of Cultural Awakening." Unpublished MA thesis, Institute of Canadian Studies, Carleton University, Ottawa, 1979.

Calnek, William Arthur. *History of the County of Annapolis*. Toronto, William Briggs, 1897; republished Belleville, Ont., Mika Publishing Company Limited, 1980.

Christie, Barbara J. "Flat Racing in Nova Scotia: Testing Ground for Horses of Stamina and Quality." *The Occasional*, VII:1 (Fall 1981), pp. 7–13; VII:2 (Spring 1982), pp. 21–25; VII:3 (Fall 1982), pp. 17–25.

Dewhurst, C. Kurt, MacDowell, Betty, and MacDowell, Marsha. *Artists in Aprons: Folk Art by American Women*. New York, E.P. Dutton in association with the Museum of American Folk Art, 1979.

Ennals, Peter, and Holdsworth, Deryck. "Vernacular Architecture and the Cultural Landscape of the Maritime Provinces – A Reconnaissance." *Atlantic Canada before Confederation, The Acadiensis Reader*, vol. 1, edited by P.A. Buckner and David Frank. Fredericton, Acadiensis Press, 1985.

Entwisle, E.A. *French Scenic Wallpapers, 1800–1860*. Leigh-on-Sea, England, F. Lewis Publishers Limited, 1972.

Field, Richard Henning. *Spirit of Nova Scotia: Traditional Decorative Folk Art, 1780–1930*. Halifax, Art Gallery of Nova Scotia. Toronto & London, Dundurn Press, 1985.

Fowler, John, and Cornforth, John. *English Decoration in the 18th Century*. London, Barrie & Jenkins, Limited, 1974.

Gignac, Gilbert L., and L'Espérance, Jeanne L. "Thoughts of Peace and Joy: A Study of the Iconography of the Croscup Room." *The Journal of Canadian Art History*, VI:2 (1982), pp. 137–78.

Greenaway, Cora. "Decorated Walls and Ceilings in Nova Scotia." *Material History Bulletin*, no. 15. Ottawa, National Museum of Man (Summer 1982), pp. 83–88.

Greenaway, Cora. "Another Painted Room." *Canadian Collector*, XVII:3 (May–June 1982), pp. 34–36.

Greenaway, Cora. *Interior Decorative Painting in Nova Scotia*. Halifax, Art Gallery of Nova Scotia, 1986.

Harper, J. Russell. *People's Art: Naïve Art in Canada*. Ottawa, National Gallery of Canada, 1973.

Harper, J. Russell. *A People's Art: Primitive, Naïve, Provincial and Folk Painting in Canada*. Toronto, University of Toronto Press, 1974.

Heritage Trust of Nova Scotia. *Seasoned Timbers: A Sampling of Historic Buildings Unique to Western Nova Scotia*. Halifax, Heritage Trust of Nova Scotia, 1972.

Hodkinson, Ian. "Conservation and Transfer of an Early 19th Century Painted Room." *The Association for Preservation Technology Bulletin*, XIV:1 (1982), pp. 17–35.

Holford, Mary. "Sesquicentennial Styles: Wearing Apparel in the Eighteen-Thirties." *Canadian Collector*, XIX:2 (Mar–Apr 1984), pp. 40–44.

Holland, Vyvyan. *Hand Coloured Fashion Plates 1770 to 1899*. London, B.T. Batsford Ltd., 1955.

Illustrated London News, The, 27 Aug 1842, front page; 3 Sep 1842, pp. 265, 296; 10 Sep 1842, p. 284; 13 Apr 1844, pp. 232, 299; 13 May 1844, p. 289; 12 Oct 1844, pp. 232–33.

Latremouille, Joann. *Pride of Home: The Working Class Housing Tradition in Nova Scotia, 1749–1949*. Hantsport, N.S., Lancelot Press Limited, 1986.

Leung, Felicity. "Wallpaper Identification Marks and the Names of Manufacturers Marketing Wallpaper in Canada." *Research Bulletin, No. 149*, Parks Canada, Nov 1980.

Leung, Felicity. *Wall Paper in Canada, 1600s–1930s*.

Microfiche Report Series No. 208. Ottawa, Parks Canada, 1983.

Lipman, Jean. *American Folk Decoration*. New York, Oxford University Press, 1951.

Lipman, Jean. *Rufus Porter, Yankee Pioneer*. New York, Clarkson N. Potter Inc., 1968.

Lipman, Jean. "Rufus Porter: Yankee Wall Painter." *Art in America*, vol. 38 (Oct 1950), pp. 135–200.

Lipman, Jean, and Winchester, Alice. *The Flowering of American Folk Art, 1776–1876*. New York, The Viking Press, 1974.

Little, Nina Fletcher. *American Decorative Wall Painting, 1700–1850*. New York, E.P. Dutton & Co. Inc., 1972.

Loudon, John Claudius. *An Encyclopædia of Cottage, Farm and Village Architecture and Furniture*. London, Longman, Rees, Orme, Brown, Green & Longman, 1833.

McClelland, Nancy. *Historic Wallpapers*. London & Philadelphia, J.P. Lippincott Company, 1924.

McGrath, Robert L. *Early Vermont Wall Paintings, 1790–1850*. Hanover, N.H., The University Press of New England, 1972.

McKendry, Blake. *Folk Art: Primitive and Naïve Art in Canada*. Toronto, Methuen Publications, 1983.

Minhinnick, Jeanne. *At Home in Upper Canada*. Toronto/Vancouver, Clarke, Irwin & Co. Ltd., 1970.

Minhinnick, Jeanne. "Some Personal Observations on the Use of Paint in Early Ontario." *The Association for Preservation Technology Bulletin*, VIII:2 (1975), pp. 13–31.

Nouvel, Odile. *Papiers peints français, 1800–1850*. Paris, Office du Livre, Éditions Vilo, 1981.

Pelletier, Gaby. *Micmac and Maliseet Decorative Traditions*. Saint John, N.B., The New Brunswick Museum, 1977.

Penner, Judith. "Michaelangelo in Overalls." *Today*, 29 May 1982, pp. 6–7, 9.

Piers, Harry. "Artists in Nova Scotia." *Collections of the Nova Scotia Historical Society*, vol. 18, Halifax, William MacNab & Son, 1914.

Porter, Rufus. *A Select Collection of Valuable and Curious Arts and Interesting Experiments*. Concord, N.H., 1826.

Porter, Rufus. "The Art of Painting." *Scientific American*, 27 weekly instalments from no. 3 (11 Sep 1845) to no. 30 (9 Apr 1846).

Scott, Barbara. "Guest of the Queen: Louis-Philippe at Windsor," Part I. *Country Life*, 10 Nov 1983, pp. 1314–16.

Scott, Barbara. "Adventures Relived: Louis-Philippe at Windsor," Part II. *Country Life*, 17 Nov 1983, pp. 1436–37.

Sparling, Mary. *Great Expectations: The European Vision in Nova Scotia, 1749–1848*. Halifax, Art Gallery, Mount Saint Vincent University, 1980.

Teynac, Françoise, Nolot, Pierre, and Vivien, Jean-Denis. *Le Monde du papier peint*. Paris, Berger-Levrault, 1981.

Townsend's Monthly Selection of Parisian Costume. London, Parisian Costume Office, no. 106 (Oct 1833).

Volpi, Charles de. *Nova Scotia: A Pictorial Record*. Toronto, Longman Canada Limited, 1974.

Vries, Leonard de. *Panorama 1842–1865: The World of the Early Victorians as Seen through the Eyes of The Illustrated London News*, London, John Murray Ltd., 1967.

Wallace, Arthur W. *An Album of Drawings of Early Buildings in Nova Scotia*. Halifax, Heritage Trust of Nova Scotia and Nova Scotia Museum, 1976.

Wallis, Wilson D., and Wallis, Ruth Sawtell. *The Micmac Indians of Eastern Canada*. Minneapolis, University of Minnesota Press, 1955.

Whitehead, Ruth Holmes. *Elitekey: Micmac Material Culture from 1600 A.D. to the Present*. Halifax, Nova Scotia Museum, 1980.

Wood, Christopher. *Victorian Panorama: Paintings of Victorian Life*. London, Faber & Faber Limited, 1976.